New NF /NF
395.22
CL7f

SEP 3 0 2008

W9-DAO-713

Fodor's

Destination Weddings

WITHDRAWN
MENASHA'S PUBLIC LIBRARY

THE
World's Most
EXTRAORDINARY
PLACES TO
Tie the Knot

E.D. SMITH PUBLIC LIBRARY

FODOR'S TRAVEL PUBLICATIONS
NEW YORK · TORONTO · LONDON · SYDNEY · AUCKLAND

WWW.FODORS.COM

Original text by Elizabeth Coggins
Project management by Bookwork Creative Associates Ltd
Design and layout: pentacorbig, UK. www.pentacorbig.co.uk
Cover design by Tigist Getachew
Copy edit by Ruth Atkinson
Americanization/edit by Diane Winkleby
Picture research by Mel Watson

Fodor's Destination Weddings
ISBN: 978-1-4000-0750-9
First edition

Published in the United States by Fodor's Travel, a division of Random House, Inc. and simultaneously
in Canada by Random House of Canada Limited, Toronto. Published in the United Kingdom by
AA Publishing.

Fodor's is a registered trademark of Random House, Inc.
Fodor's Travel is a division of Random House, Inc.

All rights reserved. Distributed by Random House, Inc., New York.
No maps, illustrations, or other portions of this book may be reproduced in any form without written
permission.

© Automobile Association Developments Limited 2007 (registered office is Fanum House, Basing View,
Basingstoke, Hampshire RG21 4EA. Registered number 1878835).

Colour separation by Keenes, Andover.
Printed and bound by Oriental Press, Dubai
10 9 8 7 6 5 4 3 2

Special sales: This book is available for special discounts for bulk purchases for sales promotions or
premiums. Special editions, including personalized covers, excerpts of existing books, and corporate
imprints, can be created in large quantities for special needs. For more information, write to Special
Markets/Premium Sales, 1745 Broadway. MD6-2, New York, NY 10019 or e-mail specialmarkets@
randomhouse.com

A03634
Mountain High Maps ® Copyright © 1993 Digital Wisdom Inc.

Important Note: Time inevitably brings changes, so always confirm prices, travel facts, and other
perishable information when it matters. Although Fodor's cannot accept responsibility for errors, you can
use this book in the confidence that we have taken care to ensure its accuracy.

Contents

Part 1 Organizing your Wedding   **6**

Choosing your Destination   *8*

Family & Friends   *10*

Be Happy—Be Healthy   *14*

Make a Smooth Getaway   *16*

Your Wedding Outfits   *20*

A Perfect Day—the Ultimate Guide to
   Bridal Beauty   *26*

Flowers, Music, Transportation & Catering   *30*

Photography & Videography   *34*

Gifts   *36*

The Ceremony   *38*

After the Wedding   *42*

Countdown to the Big Day   *44*

Destination Checklist   *49*

Part 2 Destinations   **50**

Locator Map   *52*

Bridal Files   *54*

Weather to Travel   *56*

Africa

Kenya
Malindi, *Hemingways Resort*   *60*

South Africa
Cape Town, *Mount Nelson Hotel*   *64*

Australia

New South Wales
Lord Howe Island, *Arajilla Retreat*   *70*
Sydney, *The Observatory Hotel*   *76*

Queensland
South Stradbroke Island, *Couran Cove
   Island Resort*   *80*

Europe

England
Oxford, *Le Manoir aux Quat' Saisons*   *86*

Finland
Helsinki, *Hotel Kämp*   *92*

France
French Riviera, *Château de la Chèvre d'Or*   *96*

Ireland
County Mayo, *Ashford Castle*   *100*

Italy
Venice, *Hotel Cipriani*   *104*

Scotland
Kilchrenan, *Ardanaiseig Hotel* — 110

Sweden
Jukkasjärvi, *Icehotel* — 114

Islands

Bahamas
Paradise Island, *One&Only Ocean Club* — 120

Cayman Islands
Little Cayman, *Southern Cross Club* — 124

Channel Islands
Jersey, *Longueville Manor* — 128

Cook Islands
Rarotonga, *Crown Beach Resort* — 132

Cyclades Islands, Greece
Santorini, *Hotel Katikies* — 138

Cyprus
Kouklia, *The InterContinental Aphrodite Hills Resort Hotel* — 142

Dominican Republic
Las Terrenas, *Viva Wyndham Samaná* — 146

Fiji
Viti Levu, *Outrigger on the Lagoon* — 150

Hawaii
Kauai, *Princeville Resort* — 154

Jamaica
Montego Bay, *Round Hill Hotel* — 160

Mauritius
Poste de Flacq, *One&Only Le Saint Géran* — 164
Wolmar, *Taj Exotica Resort & Spa* — 168

Nevis
Montpelier, *Montpelier Plantation Inn* — 174

North Island, New Zealand
Kaitaia, *Carrington Resort* — 178

Seychelles
Silhouette Island, *Labriz Silhouette* — 182

St. Lucia
Cap Estate, *LeSport* — 186

Thailand
Phuket, *Sheraton Grande Laguna* — 190

U.S. Virgin Islands
St. Thomas, *Wyndham Sugar Bay Resort & Spa* — 194

The Americas

Canada
Canadian Rockies, *The Fairmont Chateau Lake Louise* — 200

Mexico
Quintana Roo, *Royal Hideaway Playacar* — 206

United States
Florida, *Biltmore* — 210
Florida, *Pink Shell Beach Resort & Spa* — 214
Maryland, *The Inn at Perry Cabin* — 220
New York, *The Waldorf-Astoria* — 224
California, *The Fairmont* — 228
South Carolina, *Litchfield Plantation* — 232

Index — 236
Acknowledgments — 240

He popped the question. You decided to follow your dream and opt for a ceremony in a truly romantic destination. So let your journey commence as we guide you through the planning of your special day.

Organizing your Wedding

choosing your destination

The world's your oyster when it comes to planning a wedding abroad. Whether you dream of exchanging your vows on a sun-drenched beach with a backdrop of sparkling crystal waters and swaying palm trees, saying "I do" in some of the world's most exciting cities, or celebrating your nuptials like a princess in the dreamlike ambience of a fairytale castle—the world is full of choices.

The Caribbean is still the leader in the wedding stakes. There's a sea full of islands to choose from. Each one is different and has its own character and traits.

If you're looking for tropical destinations, there's also the sensational South Pacific and the magical islands of the Indian Ocean, which are fast escalating in popularity.

Long-haul destinations such as Australia and New Zealand are relatively new contenders in the weddings abroad market and offer a diverse choice of options.

But remember, to get the maximum enjoyment from these destinations you need to take at least a three-week vacation.

Couples seeking a taste of adventure could do no better than to choose to walk on the wild side by combining a beach and safari wedding and honeymoon in Africa. For an Asian experience, Thailand with its golden pagodas and exotic islands is an idyllic place to tie the knot.

The Americas provide one of the most diverse, spectacular, and pulsating backdrops for marriages.

From the legendary cities of New York and San Francisco, the sun-drenched, celebrated coast of Florida, and old-world colonial charm of Maryland and South Carolina to the vibrance that is Mexico and the stunning beauty of the Canadian Rockies—all are packed with an endless array of wonders for a traveling twosome.

Throughout the centuries Europe has enticed some of the world's greatest lovers with its iconic charm, its sights, culture, and the romantic ambience of a bygone age.

Europe offers the choice of coastal, island, and city destinations, each as alluring as the next. In Sweden you can find the most incredible venue in the world—a beautiful palace carved out of ice.

The British Isles offer couples the chance to share in an amazing long history with destinations ranging from Norman manor houses set in perfumed English country gardens to majestic castles set amid some of the world's most beautiful countryside and coastal regions.

One of the simplest ways of tying the knot abroad is by taking advantage of one of the many all-inclusive wedding and honeymoon packages offered by tour operators. Depending on the type of package, these include administration costs together with items such as photographs, flowers, and the cake. If you want added extras, such as photographs at sunset, music, videos, and exotic transportation, these can be arranged for an additional fee.

Most travel companies will have a dedicated wedding department based in your own country, and there will be a wedding coordinator onsite to make sure everything runs smoothly and to deal with any problems you may have. The wedding coordinator can arrange for you both to spend the night before the wedding in different rooms or hotels if desired, advise you on the best hair and beauty salons at the destination, and even organize witnesses for you.

If you want to make your own arrangements or have a wedding in a destination or hotel that isn't listed in the many dedicated wedding brochures, then most hotels have a wedding coordinator who will guide you through the whole process and help you arrange your special day.

But do remember before you start your planning to check with the consulate or embassy of your chosen destination about the legalities, documents required, length of residence, and general procedures for marriages. Some countries have very strict and complicated rules governing weddings and the issuing of licenses, so it's wise to be clear right from the start just exactly what planning you need to do.

family & friends

A wedding in a local church has been looked upon for generations as the traditional way of getting married. But today marrying in a romantic hideaway, thousands of miles away from home is appealing more and more to couples who want to escape the familiar, and jet off and tie the knot in an unusual and romantic or exotic setting.

Escaping to a different setting is also the perfect chance to kiss the stress of planning a large wedding goodbye, and eliminate the problem of awkward relatives and competitive in-laws. Second-time-arounders find this a welcome option as they avoid the memories another church wedding can rekindle.

One of the greatest pleasures of getting married is sharing your day with your family and friends. Many couples say there is nothing to beat the atmosphere created by having loved ones around to give them a touch of tender loving care and support as they prepare for making the vows that will last a lifetime.

It's also an opportunity to catch up with friends and relatives who you haven't seen for some time. And, of course, for the couple's parents it's a highly emotional experience and the important stage in parenthood as they see their son or daughter finally flee the nest to set up their own home.

That's why it's important before finally deciding on a ceremony abroad to spend some time reflecting on your wedding and what marriage means to you. One of the prime factors to consider is that getting married abroad will preclude many of your friends and relatives from attending your wedding. Of course this might be the very reason for choosing a remote location, but nevertheless it's an important issue that has to be considered.

Ask yourself some searching questions. Will you regret not having some members of your immediate family with you on the most special day of your life? Will they feel upset at not being able to share in this precious moment? Will you be able to cope emotionally with being isolated within a resort or hotel in a strange and unfamiliar environment with no one to turn to to calm those pre-wedding nerves?

Although it may seem a romantic adventure at the time, some brides admit later that they felt lonely and even sad at not having their nearest and dearest there to "hold their hand," and share in the excitement. Many mothers tell of feeling heartbroken, hurt, or shunned because they were not able to share in the emotion of their child's big day.

Many couples overcome this problem by taking all of their immediate family with them to their wedding destination.

But before you contemplate this, consider how you'll feel about sharing your husband and honeymoon with the rest of your family.

The perfect option is to choose a two-center honeymoon. You can spend the days leading up to the wedding in one resort with your family and friends, and then take off for another resort or an island retreat after the wedding.

If this isn't practical, then another solution is to transfer to another hotel for your wedding night and the rest of your honeymoon. You can then arrange to meet your family for lunch or dinner when the mood takes you.

Many couples find marrying abroad the ideal solution. Tying the knot is often just a formality if you have been in a relationship for some time.

Sneaking away to get married and telling everyone afterward is the ideal scenario. Likewise incorporating the wedding and honeymoon into one time frame is an idyllic option for couples with pressured careers and hectic workloads who want to maximize their quality time together.

Destination weddings also appeal to couples marrying for the second time. Being thousands of miles away from your own, familiar environment in a new and exciting place is unlikely to evoke memories of your previous wedding ceremony. The low-key ceremony associated with marriages abroad also provides the intimacy and privacy that many divorced or widowed couples seek, yet it still enables them to celebrate their vows in a romantic, personal setting rather than the stark formality of a courthouse office.

Marrying abroad is also the answer for couples with different opinions about how a marriage should be celebrated. You may yearn for a glamorous ceremony with all the frills and formalities while your partner may envisage a simple, private, no-frills affair. Tying the knot in a romantic destination enables you and your partner to live your dream and enjoy the best of both worlds.

When you're deciding to get married abroad, do remember that services and facilities will be different from those at home. Although staff at the vast majority of resorts speak English, when it comes to dealing with problems, you may occasionally come across someone who isn't fluent enough to understand your instructions, and it may take time to find another member of staff with a better understanding of English.

Hair and beauty services may be different from what you are used to. Remember that in some parts of the world, where stronger colors are fashionable and the norm, the natural bridal look isn't always achievable or even desirable.

Also don't be surprised if the flowers you receive are different from flowers at home and appear bright and gaudy; they will look good as part of the big picture. And speaking of pictures, the resort's photographer may not have sophisticated lighting and equipment, but you can check their work before the service.

And finally, a wedding in paradise doesn't have to stop your friends and family from sharing your joy at a later date. Have a big party when you arrive home and invite friends and family to relive the happiest day of your life.

be happy—be healthy

The beautiful white sandy beaches and blue skies of exotic destinations can spell magic for those who are getting married abroad. But sun, sea, and sand coupled with the climate and native food can also spell a health hazard for the unprepared traveler. So if you want to enjoy every minute of your dream wedding and honeymoon abroad, it's essential that you take health precautions.

Immunization and Vaccination

These requirements vary from country to country. Malaria protection is usually required for most destinations in Asia, South America, India and the Indian Ocean, and Africa. Yellow fever protection is also compulsory for certain South American and African destinations.

All these requirements vary from time to time so it's advisable to check with your doctor or travel clinic at least three months before you go.

Remember to check how long beforehand you need to have the injections, as some will be a single dose while others require a course.

Long-haul Flights

If you are flying long haul, make your journey safe and healthy. The more precautions you take, the better you will feel on your flight. Move around frequently during the flight to stretch your legs and maintain healthy circulation.

In the seat pockets, most airlines provide details of recommended exercises that can be done in your seat to help your circulation and avoid cramps, joint stiffness, and other aches and pains caused by sitting through a long-haul flight.

Make sure you drink plenty of fluids, particularly water, to keep hydrated, and avoid drinking too much alcohol. Don't sit with your legs crossed, and don't wear tight pants, jeans, or clothing that is too restrictive. Investing in a pair of flight socks may not seem a romantic option, but they may help protect you against deep vein thrombosis (DVT) and are effective in preventing swollen ankles and feet.

Food for Thought

Sampling exotic foods may be exciting, but with different standards of hygiene it's wise to exercise caution, especially in the case of raw vegetables, shellfish, drinking water, and ice in drinks.

If you do develop severe diarrhea and/or vomiting, you need to seek medical advice. A hot climate plus loss of body fluids could easily result in you becoming dehydrated.

Also remember that if you are taking the contraceptive pill and you have severe diarrhea and vomiting, the pill's effectiveness will be reduced and shouldn't be relied upon as a safe method of contraception. So an essential inclusion in your suitcase is, yes, you've guessed, condoms.

Spray Away

Enjoying a romantic stroll through wooded areas may not be the ideal party for two that you had in mind when insects decide to join you.

So remember to pack an insect repellent spray and to cover up. If you are prone to reaction from insect bites, make sure that you take a course of antihistamine pills before you go away and also take some antihistamine cream and pills with you.

A good tip for beating the bugs is to keep covered up in really hot, humid climates where mosquitoes and other flying insects abound.

Mosquitoes are usually the most common type of biting insect. To prevent being bitten, apply an insect repellent and cover up exposed skin with full-length pants, socks, and long sleeves when you are outside.

In malarial areas, dusk to dawn is the highest risk period for contracting malaria so make sure you frequently apply repellent.

When you go to bed, either sleep under a net or in an air-conditioned room that is insect-free. You must also take malaria pills.

Do remember to shake clothes out before dressing to make sure there are no insects caught in your clothing. Apply your insect repellent sparingly to exposed skin only and never apply to irritated or broken skin. Keep your sprays in a cool place, and if the worst comes to the worst, and you do get a bite, keep an eye on it to ensure it doesn't become septic.

Sun Aware

Don't spoil your trip of a lifetime by getting burned. Take it easy, build up the time you're exposed to the sun, and protect skin at all times by using a high SPF cream suitable for your skin type.

Cover up, wear a wide-brimmed hat, and loose layered clothing. Remember you can still burn when it's cloudy, when you are swimming, or even in the shade.

Never underestimate the effects of the sun on the skin. The risk of skin cancer is greatest if you burn. Sunburn is skin damage. On the surface it peels away, but deep down the damage remains and a few doses of sunburn could lead to skin cancer in later years.

If you do burn, cover up immediately. If you blister and it bursts, your skin may become infected so medical advice should be sought.

Feel good and feel safe. The warmth of the sun makes us happy, healthy, relaxed, and alive. Enjoy these positive good feelings without the ill effects of overexposure.

make a smooth getaway

Planning and packing for what will perhaps be the biggest trip of your life is a task that is often left until the last minute, and the result is you seem to have packed all of your wardrobe but still don't have the right outfits when you get to your destination. Your big toilet bag weighs you down, your special outfit and his suit are hideously crumpled, and your sun hat is squashed beyond all recognition.

Successful packing, the kind where your personal effects emerge unscathed and you have enough of them to last the trip, is an art. But it's an art that can easily be learned.

Identify Your Essentials

You will obviously need toiletries, clothes, sun preparations, shoes, cameras, and sunglasses. If you're staying in a hotel, you can leave out things like travel irons and hairdryers, as these are usually provided, but check in advance to make sure your room is fully equipped. Next preplan your wardrobe and look for items that will double up.

- A sundress can be worn with flat shoes or sandals during the day, with heels and jewelry for the evening, and even with pants as a tunic for either day or evening.
- A sarong skirt can be worn in the day with a T-shirt or blouse, over a swimsuit on the beach, or in the evening with a camisole or bodice.
- Large, very light squares of fabric are incredibly versatile. Use one as a beach cover-up over the hips, tied over your bust as a dress, tied around your neck and waist to make a halter top, or draped over a simple slip dress as a scarf for evening.
- A cotton sweater can double as a jacket for evening, while a linen-blend pant suit can be dressed up or down with pieces worn separately.
- A scarf is a useful accessory. Wear a small, square bandanna to protect your hair on the beach or tie it around your neck with a shirt. A chiffon scarf is great for evenings, tied around your hips or worn around the shoulders. Cotton scarves also protect against the sun on the beach or while sightseeing.

- If you want to make a special purchase for your honeymoon, make it a swimsuit or bikini. As well as looking great when you are in the pool or the ocean, a well-thought-out swimsuit can double as a top for the evening, especially at a beach resort.

Many women find it difficult to leave shoes at home, packing for every footwear eventuality. Unless you plan to do a lot of walking, or are going on an adventure trip, three pairs of shoes should be enough. A pair of light, heeled shoes or sandals for evening, canvas espadrilles or light trainers, and some flat leather sandals will suffice, along with a pair of slippers. You may want to add water-resistant shoes such as flip-flops for the beach.

Purses are another weak point. Resist the temptation to pack lots just in case, and try to limit yourself to three.

Start with a large leather tote bag for your trip, shopping, and day trips. If you're a sightseeing couple, you may want to take a backpack. Next, find a big straw or canvas beach bag that will fold flat in your suitcase.

Then choose a pretty clutch or beaded bag that coordinates with your evening or wedding clothes and you will be ready for anything. Your evening bag can also double as a pouch to pack your jewelry in while you travel.

Double Up

Don't weigh yourself down with lots of cosmetics and toiletries for your honeymoon. Most couples go away for two or three weeks at the most, and travel-size products will last that long.

Most brands do travel-size products. Check out tiny packages that give you just enough for a few weeks. Testers and trial sizes are ideal. Before you pack, check airline restrictions on cosmetics and liquids in carryon and tote bags.

Alternatively, you may want to decant your favorite products so you can be sure your skin won't suffer while you are away. Travel bottles and jars can be bought in department stores and pharmacies.

Don't take two products when one will do. Try a shampoo that can also be used as a body wash or a cleanser that also tones and refreshes your face. Invest in a body moisturizer that incorporates a shimmering element that will look great in the evening.

A wide range of makeup products can also be used for more than one function. Look out for gels that can be used on cheeks and lips, sticks that are eyeshadows and blushers in one, and powders that can be used to highlight almost anywhere.

Perfect Packing

Take out some of the chance element and check the weather at your destination before you start packing so you know the temperatures and conditions you can expect. Then make a list of everything you will need, including clothes, toiletries, medicines, and things that are essential for your trip.

Put the things that have to go into your hand luggage to one side, remembering to include any electrical items that most airlines insist are kept with you, as well as anything valuable or fragile.

Check off each item on your list as you pack it, and don't be tempted to add extras along the way.

Start with heavy items and shoes, which should be packed in plastic bags at the bottom of the case. Fill the toes of your shoes with socks and other small items to use the spare space. Then roll casual clothes, linen items, and sweaters, as they will crease less. These rolls can then be used to protect any fragile items.

Pack jars, tubes, and anything liquid-filled or runny in small plastic bags—freezer bags are ideal—as you don't want to arrive at your destination with your clothes covered in toothpaste!

It's better to pack individual items in small bags rather than putting them in a toilet bag, as you will be able to use them to fill the gaps between other items.

Evening clothes can be packed between layers of plastic, the modern equivalent of tissue paper, and kept as flat as possible.

There is an equally important list of things not to pack. If you're taking any valuable jewelry, it's safer to wear it or keep it on your person on the journey (this applies to your wedding bands too). Put jewelry in the hotel safe on your arrival.

Don't pack all the sweaters you need for your trip. Temperatures can drop quite quickly on a plane, so have a warm layer available in your hand luggage, especially if you're on a night flight.

Finally, it's sensible to pack some toiletries and a light change of clothes in your hand luggage, in case the worst happens and your luggage decides to head off to a different destination from the one you've chosen.

The Wedding Wardrobe

Because you're marrying abroad, the most important part of your luggage will be your wedding outfit. Each airline has its own procedures for transporting large garments such as wedding gowns. However, do remember that in all events your outfit will be classed as part of your luggage allowance so you may have to reduce your luggage accordingly. Do make a point of checking with your airline about its particular policy in regard to the way wedding outfits are carried.

Special Measures

The clothes that you wear for the ceremony need to be in as good a condition as you can possibly get them.

All eyes will be on you, and the photographs that are taken will last a lifetime.

It's worth mentioning to the suppliers of your dress and of the groom's outfit that you intend to take them to foreign climes for the ceremony, as the experts will be able to suggest fabrics and designs that are suitable for these conditions.

The groom's suit or outfit should be quite simple to pack. If there's no hanging space on the plane, pack the suit as flat as you can in a large suitcase. Try to put it on top of the case, as layers of clothes will cause creasing. Arrangements to press the suit can be made with the hotel when you arrive at the destination.

The best time to pack your wedding dress is at the final purchase. Ask the designer or bridal outfitter to fold and pack your wedding dress for you in tissue paper, and then put it into your suitcase if this is the way you are going to carry it. If you're using a hanging cover, protect the garment by wrapping it in a cotton sheet and then in plastic before zipping it in the cover. When you arrive at your destination, take the dress out of the case or holder and hang it so the fabric is as free as possible. This way, most, if not all, the creases should drop out. If there's a major problem, ask the hotel's valeting service for help. Make sure you know the fabric that your dress is made of so it can be treated properly.

Hats are often difficult to pack. The best solution is to put the hat in a rigid case and pack clothes around it to protect it from too much damage. First, stuff the crown with underwear or light clothing. If the hat has a brim, pack this out too and then place it onto some folded garments in your suitcase. Then build around the hat with other soft clothing. This is much better than struggling with a fragile, cardboard hat box on the plane and risking it being damaged in the overhead bin.

your wedding outfits

What you choose to wear for your wedding is a highly individual choice. As you have chosen to marry abroad, you should plan accordingly when it comes to fabrics and the general logistics of having to transport your wedding outfits to your destination.

The Wedding Wardrobe

It's your special day and you will have your own ideas about how you want to look. Don't be bullied into choosing a dress that is plain, simple, and deemed as something suitable for weddings abroad if you want to look like a fairytale princess.

But do take into account the temperature and the surroundings of your destination and tailor your dream dress accordingly.

Above all you need to feel comfortable and confident on your wedding day. Choose natural fabrics if it's a hot climate and try to avoid tight-fitting bodices.

If you've opted for a castle or the grand salon of a hotel, think of the surroundings. You may want to choose a dress that reflects the period of the venue such as medieval, Elizabethan, Victorian, or even the elegant 1920s; or the culture of the country, such as Mexican national dress.

Nothing is worse than a shivering bride. So if you're holding your ceremony in a cooler climate, consider a cloak or coat which can be removed once you are inside the venue. Even in warmer climates it can become chilly as the sun goes down, so ask your bridal designer to create a wrap to cover your shoulders. A wrap is also useful as protection against the sun if you're taking a carriage or boat ride after the ceremony.

In warmer climes avoid strappy, sandal-type shoes as these can cut into the feet—choose low-heeled pumps or shoes with a small heel, preferably in a fabric.

The first step when choosing your dress is to analyze your figure. Only a tiny majority of brides have perfect proportions. Your shape is part of what makes you who you are, and you should aim to accentuate its best features while minimizing its less wonderful ones.

Look critically at yourself in a mirror. Be realistic about your figure and look for its positive points. Do you have beautiful shoulders, a small waist, long legs, elegant ankles? Then examine your worst points—perhaps thin arms or larger hips. When you've done this, make mental notes and bear them in mind when you see your bridal designer, or go shopping.

At your first appointment with your designer, or when you visit a bridal store, discuss what styles you have in mind and what parts of your figure you want to emphasize. Be open-minded and listen to any suggestions.

You may have envisaged yourself in a long dress, but after trying on some shorter ones you may change your mind. But don't be bullied into having a dress in a design or fabric you don't feel one hundred percent comfortable in.

FIGURE IT OUT

Broad Shoulders
Go for

Thin, spaghetti straps

V- or scoop necklines

Halter necks

Avoid

Broad, wide-set straps

Details on the shoulder, e.g., frills,
flowers, gathers

Narrow Shoulders
Go for

Thick, wide-set straps

Wide, horizontal necklines

Puff sleeves

Avoid

Halter necks

Cut-away shoulders

Very low, v- or scoop necklines

Large Hips or Thighs
Go for

Plain matte fabrics

Vertical seams on skirts

Details on top half to draw the
eye upwards

Avoid

Bias-cut dresses

Gathers at hip or thigh level

Bows and flowers on hips, tummy,
and behind

Tall Brides
Go for

Layered styles

Horizontal details

Wide dress styles

Avoid

Very slim styles

Vertical lines

High headdresses

Petite Brides
Go for

Slim silhouette

Details or decoration on top half

Plain bottom half

Avoid

Very large details, e.g., flowers
and bows

Wide sleeves

Decoration at floor level

Fuller-figured Brides
Go for

Simple styles in matte fabrics

Medium to low necklines

Vertical style lines

Avoid

Frills, flounces, and puff sleeves

Very high necklines

Shiny fabrics

Clingy fabrics

The Undercover Story

What you wear beneath your dress
is critical to how you look on your
wedding day. Underwear has to
fit well, be suitable for the design
and fabric of your dress, and be
comfortable enough to see you
through the day and into your
evening celebrations.

The lingerie you choose
should enhance and accentuate
your figure, and make you feel
completely and utterly at ease.
If you're marrying in a hot climate,
it's particularly important that you
choose a natural fabric such as
cotton that will keep you cool and
comfortable. You should avoid
synthetic fibers.

The style and fabric of your
wedding dress should dictate
the type of lingerie you wear, and
therefore they should be chosen
in tandem.

The majority of bridal designers
and stockists strongly recommend
that your lingerie be bought when
you've made your choice of dress
and then brought along to every
fitting, ensuring that both dress and
underwear work together.

Before you even begin to make
your choice of lingerie for your big
day, have yourself professionally
measured. It's a fact that most
women wear the wrong size bra.

This alone can contribute to an uncomfortable fit and an unflattering line. Put yourself in the hands of a capable, trained fitter at your favorite lingerie shop or department store, and trust her judgment.

When you start choosing your lingerie, remember that, almost above all else, comfort is crucial. Your wedding day will involve movement (everything from climbing into a car, horse-drawn carriage, or even a canoe if you are marrying in the South Pacific) as well as standing for a long period of time. If you don't feel that the garments you're considering will stand up to the rigors of the day, don't even think of buying them.

Choose fabrics that will allow maximum movement and feel good against your skin, while making sure that the garments are breathable.

Take into account the fabric and design of your dress. The fabric's density will dictate the color choice of your lingerie. Pure white is good under opaque material, while ivory and pearl are perfect partners for lace and chiffon. However, the ideal color for any lingerie is skintone; generally the darker the tone, the less visible the lingerie.

Ask your designer or bridal store for their opinion on which lingerie finish will work the best, as it's the choice of finish—whether matte or shiny—that will encourage your wedding gown to be well-behaved. Nothing looks worse than two textures that are completely at loggerheads with each other.

Be conscious of where your underwear finishes in relation to your dress. Beware of intrusive straps, visible back fastenings, detectable panty line, lace that refuses to lie flat, or peeps over the edge of your dress. You don't want to be worried about having things showing, or worse, visible in your favorite wedding photograph.

Well Suited

Whether soaking up the sun on a tropical beach, relaxing by the pool, or splashing around in the pristine blue waters of your paradise island —swimwear is an important part of your honeymoon wardrobe.

Ideally, you should invest in at least four pieces of swimwear—a quick-drying one piece for serious swimming, a couple of bikinis for sunbathing, and a glamorous two piece or one piece for those memorable poolside parties and beach-bar discos.

But before taking the plunge and buying your swimwear, you need to be honest with yourself if you want to look your best.

A swimsuit more than any other garment needs to fit well and flatter your shape. If it's not flattering in the fitting room, it will look a hundred times worse in the glare of bright sunshine on the beach.

If you're larger than a B cup, choose styles with sized cups. These are designed to fit like a bra and have either underwired cups or softer, less-structured support.

Higher backs or crossed straps will also help with support, and wider straps will help with comfort.

To draw attention away from the bust, select a suit or bikini with print or detail at the bottom.

Small-busted beach babes should select styles with bust detail or padding. Feminine shapes will flatter and add definition. Draw attention to the bust by choosing styles that use bold prints or color.

Don't opt for a high-cut leg shape unless you have the perfect figure. A medium-cut leg will lengthen the leg but minimize the hips, especially in a dark color. If you have heavy thighs, avoid styles that cut into your legs.

For those with larger hips, drawing attention away from the hips with bust detail or ruching balances the body. Choose a two piece with a deep pant. A dark color or vertical stripes will lengthen the leg.

If you're in the larger-size bracket, opt for a panelled swimsuit with a control element that helps shape. Steer clear of fussy detail, but don't choose anything drab. Strong bold prints will break up the body line—vertical stripes are good, as are chevron styles. Avoid low-cut legs, which can dig into your thighs.

With the right swimsuit you can also achieve the perfect body line.

Styles with high legs and low necklines will reduce the body length, while a lower leg line will make the body look longer. Vertical stripes and plunging necklines will also elongate the body and you can create curves with frills, ruching, and embossed fabrics.

TOP 10 TIPS FOR GROOMS

1 If the bride is wearing a formal traditional gown, then opt for a tuxedo or suit. If she has chosen a more modern, casual look, then your outfit should be in harmony with this: your outfit should complement your bride's.

2 Try to imagine how you want to look in the wedding photographs, as these will be with you for the rest of your life. Consider a variety of outfits for your wedding abroad. For a formal look, stylish four-button single-breasted suits, Nehru jackets, or tuxedos look good. For a casual look, try a collarless shirt and lightweight trousers with a vest, or a white tuxedo teamed with designer jeans.

3 Choose appropriate material. Although linen is cool it's also creaseable, so steer clear. Before you even leave your room, you could end up with a hideously wrinkled outfit. Remember to pack warm clothes for cooler destinations.

4 If you're wearing a vest, make sure you have enough room to breathe after all the champagne and the rich food. Trying it on a few weeks before the wedding and having a snug fit probably means that it will be tight on the big day.

5 Your vest should be long enough to cover the waistband of your trousers. Ensure that it doesn't show any shirt when you raise your arms above your head. Always leave the bottom button undone.

6 When you buy your shirt, make sure you can fit a finger down the front of the collar, as on the day anxiety may cause you to expand slightly. Wear a wing collar to add formality.

7 Make sure your shirt is washed and ironed before the day. This will take out the unironable lines that occur with flat-packed shirts and will make it soft and comfortable.

8 Check trousers are the correct length so they don't look untidy, and that jacket cuffs allow for shirt cuffs to be seen.

9 Buy shoes at least a month before the wedding and wear them in. Blisters are no fun when walking down the aisle. Consider what will match your outfit. Ankle boots or slip-on shoes won't catch the bottom of your trousers, and will give a smooth line. To avoid problems wear your wedding shoes to trouser fittings.

10 Have a manicure the day before the wedding and a haircut at least a week before, just in case there are any mistakes.

a perfect day—the ultimate guide to bridal beauty

In the run-up to your wedding, it's not just your face you have to take care of—it's your whole body. Start a revitalization program with some gentle exercise and making sure you drink plenty of water. Regular exercise helps the body's fat reserves convert into energy, giving you a more streamlined shape. A simple program of gentle activities such as walking, swimming, or biking can be built into your weekly activities without your even noticing it.

Relax Your Senses

Make sure you take time out each day to relax. Two easy techniques, which even the busiest bride can fit into her routine, include closing your eyes and counting backward from 20, saying each number silently as you breathe out. Repeat this simple exercise twice. Alternatively, shut your eyes and imagine a tranquil scene. Hold this in your mind for five minutes without letting other thoughts intrude. Once you are relaxed, indulge in some home pampering aromatherapy treatments.

Scrub Up

Get into the habit of using a gentle exfoliating body scrub or cream two or three times a week to remove dull surface cells. Exfoliation gives the skin a finer texture, boosting circulation while softening areas such as heels,

knees, and elbows that are prone to dry skin and looking unsightly.

Big Softie

There are hundreds of body creams and lotions, but if you prefer to use something a little less greasy, then a dry oil is for you. Used daily after bathing or showering it enhances

skin softness and prevents dehydration. One of the best treatments for your skin is to drink several glasses of water each day.

Happy Hands

The spotlight is on your hands on your wedding day so don't neglect them. Get into the habit of massaging your hands with a rich moisture cream for five minutes every night to nourish the parched cells. A good tip is to wear a pair of cotton gloves in bed to keep the moisture close to the skin. Apply a cream in the morning to protect the skin and prevent moisture loss. During the summer use a cream with UV filters or an SPF factor.

Give your hands a "facial" once a week by exfoliating them with a special hand scrub, followed by a mask especially for the hands.

Book yourself a manicure before the wedding.

Sensational Skin

Your skin reflects your inner health, so if you don't look after your body, your complexion will be the first to suffer. Start by looking at your diet. Overloading with alcohol, coffee, tea, processed food, and a poor input of essential nutrients leaves skin looking dull, lifeless, and all too often covered in blemishes.

Add to this an overdose of pre-wedding stress, lack of sleep, fresh air and exercise, and you could end up with skin problems.

Skincare plays a vital part in creating a clear complexion. So where do you start?

Drinking lots of water is vital for good skin, and cleansing is another important aspect. Clean your skin twice a day—more may cause irritation. Make sure you deep cleanse once a month, or more if your skin is oily. Remember to always use a cleanser to complement your skin type.

Exfoliation is an important part of your daily skincare regime as skin is constantly producing new cells and shedding old ones. Exfoliators slough off these dead cells on the surface and leave skin smoother, more radiant, and more even in color so makeup sits better and lasts longer.

Finally, use a toner to refresh, close the pores, and remove any excess oil. Choose your toner in tandem with your skin type. If your skin is dry or sensitive, you should choose a gentle alcohol-free toner.

Skin needs moisture constantly. Apply this every time after cleansing and toning. To top up levels of moisture in the skin, invest in a special hydrating cream to use alongside your favorite moisturizer.

To complete your skincare program have a weekly mini facial using a treatment mask. Oily skins benefit from a deep-pore cleansing mask. Dry and normal skins need moisturizing and hydrating masks.

Five Steps to Clear Skin

Drink four to six glasses of water a day to keep your skin hydrated.

In the morning drink a cup of hot water with the juice of half a lemon. Add some honey if you feel this is a little sour for your taste.

Replace tea and coffee with herbal teas. Rosehip is rich in vitamin C.

Nourish skin daily by basing your diet on fresh nutritious foods: fruit, vegetables, beans, brown rice, wholegrain breads, and natural yogurts, supplemented with nuts, sunflower seeds, grilled fish, chicken, and lean meat.

Don't drink more than two glasses of wine per day and avoid hard liquor.

Your Crowning Glory

All hair types are affected by climate changes, particularly humidity when the air is full of moisture, causing the strands to swell and expand. The moisture can weigh down fine hair leaving it looking flat and limp, while hair that is prone to curling will become fluffy and frizzy. Preventing excess moisture from penetrating the hair shaft in a humid climate is important.

You can do this by using a conditioning treatment or leave-in conditioner for the mid-lengths to the ends of your hair, which will seal the tips. Follow this by applying a little serum to the ends.

If you sunbathe or swim prior to your wedding, do be aware of the damaging effects of salt, chlorine, and sand in particular, as they all roughen the surface of the hair, leaving it dull, damaged, and porous. Always protect your hair with a UV protection spray.

When choosing your wedding hairstyle don't be persuaded into having a style that you don't feel comfortable with. You know what suits you, and your wedding abroad is not the time to opt for dramatic changes. Chat to your hair stylist about styles that will complement your face shape, body shape, and your own personality.

21 WAYS TO BEAT THE HEAT

If you're getting married in a hot climate, you have to consider certain steps.

1. Go easy on sunbathing in the days before your wedding and wear a high SPF sunscreen. You don't want to look like a boiled lobster in your wedding photographs.

2. Cool down in the heat by spritzing your face with mineral water or a refreshing spray. Keep it in the refrigerator and spray lightly to refresh your skin and makeup.

3. If your skin is inclined to be oily, use a purifying cleansing gel to remove the excess oil that causes shine.

4. If the worst comes to the worst and you do start to shine, take a leaf out of granny's book and use some oil-blotting sheets.

5. To stop T-zone shine, invest in a matifying cream or gel.

6. To protect against dark undereye circles from crying or sweating, invest in some waterproof mascara and eyeliner.

7. Choose lipsticks and nail polishes in brighter, stronger colors than you normally would for a wedding at home. In tropical climes the light is much brighter, and pale, neutral colors tend to look insipid, especially with a tan.

8. Pamper those tootsies. Pack a cooling, refreshing footspray.

9. Barefoot brides need to pretty-up their toe nails with vibrant funky varnish. Use a top coat to protect against unsightly chipping.

10. Heat and long flights can cause your feet and your legs to swell. Cool and soothe them with a refreshing leg gel or energizing emulsion.

11. You want to look radiant in your photos, so don't go barefaced. You need foundation and color to define your features and make you look really glamorous. Choose an oil-free foundation with an SPF factor.

12. To avoid your eye color sliding and creasing use a waterproof product.

13. To give your makeup the ultimate staying power apply a little serum underneath your foundation.

14. Allow your foundation to dry thoroughly before applying loose powder. Dust lightly with a large brush and then dust again to avoid the flour-bag look.

15. Use a lipgloss or lipstick with an SPF factor, and to keep those lips kissable apply a slick of sunscreen over the color.

16. Choose a moisturizer with an SPF factor to protect your face against the sun and the elements.

17. Excessive heat and long-haul flights dehydrate your skin, so invest in a hydrating mask. Use at regular intervals in the week leading up to your flight, and then use on alternate days when you get to your destination.

18. If you have dry skin, it will dehydrate very quickly, especially in a hot climate, so use a hydrating cream at least once a day under your moisturizer to put back the water that the heat will take out.

19. When the heat is on, alcohol-free fragrances are the best choice as alcohol can sometimes cause sensitivity and mark the skin. Perfumes and preparations with strong fragrances also attract insects, especially at night.

20. Choose an after-sun cream with an anti-mosquito formula to moisturize your skin, particularly in the evening.

21. Finally, allow yourself plenty of time to shower, cool down, run through your skincare routine, apply your makeup, and get ready for the ceremony. Rushing around will only make you hot and flustered. Just breathe and enjoy!

flowers, music, transportation & catering

Flowers, music, transportation, and catering are all elements that will add to the magic of your special day. Part of the excitement of getting married abroad is that some things might have to be left to the last minute to select. It isn't always possible to see exactly what your options are, until you arrive at your chosen venue and have your first face-to-face meeting with your wedding coordinator.

If you have firm ideas about exactly what you want, most wedding coordinators will, if humanly possible, be able to address your particular requirements. But do give them plenty of advance warning. They aren't magicians and it may take time to source and order what you want.

Flower Power

However large or small, your bridal bouquet is a centerpiece on your wedding day, particularly as you walk up the aisle or across a tropical beach, and pose for photographs after the ceremony.

Your flowers should complement your dress as well as your figure. But don't expect to have the same choice of flowers as you would at home. In tropical climes, flowers will be brighter and even appear gaudy, but this adds to the exotic atmosphere of a wedding day in paradise.

There are no hard-and-fast rules, but certain bouquet shapes tend to suit particular dress styles. A traditional full-skirted dress looks best with a long, trailing cascade bouquet. For a straight, sheath-style dress, a small hand-tied nosegay is more suitable. If you have chosen a princess or empire-line dress, then opt for a round nosegay arrangement with tendrils tapering to a point that follows the line of your skirt. A simple, modern dress looks good with a single-stem arrangement or a tightly packed nosegay with a sculpted profile.

You will have undoubtedly chosen a dress to best flatter your figure, so if you select flowers to match your dress, they will complement your body curves.

Petite brides often think carrying a long bouquet will make them look taller, but it won't. The perfect choice is a simple, round bouquet that is not too big. Tall brides look amazing with bouquets trailing to the ground or carrying a single-stem flower, while bigger brides look stunning with large flamboyant bouquets.

If you're wearing a fresh flower headdress do make sure you feel comfortable in it. If you're also wearing a veil, the flowers shouldn't be attached to it. Make sure the flowers are pinned directly into the hair and the veil attached by combs.

Ideally the flowers for the groom's boutonniere should match flowers from the bride's bouquet. The bride's bouquet should also set the style for the flowers carried by your bridesmaids. If your attendants are too young to cope with carrying a bouquet then have flower hoops or an arrangement in a basket.

Do ask to see the floral displays for both the ceremony and reception. These are usually appropriate to the setting, but it may be possible to organize alternative arrangements.

Flowers placed on tables at the wedding celebration dinner or your post-nuptial party should be carefully positioned so that they don't obstruct people's view.

If you're using candles in your table centerpieces, vary their height, with half tall and half small.

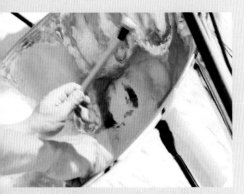

Music Please, Maestro

The music you choose will set the scene for your special day and make it memorable—live music will make it unforgettable. One of the best things about marrying abroad is the option of having traditional music played by local bands or musicians. Whether it's a steel band, calypso singer, piper, mariachi band, warrior drums, or a choir of Buddhist monks, it all adds to the wonder of your wedding.

The amount and type of music you include in your ceremony is a personal choice. It's perfectly possible to have a ceremony with no music or to employ live musicians for various times during your special day.

Stately homes and the grand salons of hotels and castles lend themselves well to string quartets, harpists, classical singers, or piano music. Some older buildings insist on live music, as the vibrations from recorded music can damage the structure, so do check this before arranging your music.

If you're having recorded music, check that there's a sound system available and that it's of a reasonable quality. If it's a little crackly, ask if it's possible to rent a system to give the sound you want.

Before hiring your final choice of music, it's wise to hear the performers play. Ask your wedding coordinator if there's a CD or tape available, or where you can hear the musicians perform in the days leading up to your wedding.

Transportation

As you will probably be marrying in the confines of your hotel, transportation is no problem—you can hotfoot it to the wedding ceremony. However, in some places in the South Pacific, a bride can arrive by warrior canoe.

Although this sounds romantic, do consider your dress and getting in and out of the boat. If possible have a rehearsal before the big day if you want to avoid going overboard.

If you do need transportation to the ceremony, limousines are a good option as they accommodate wide dresses and you're less likely to arrive creased and wrinkled. Vintage cars are a stylish choice, but remember they are gas-guzzling, have very little room for large dresses, and even the most reliable vehicle can be prone to breakdowns.

Horse-and-carriage rides are romantic but can be bumpy. Brides often find getting into the carriage difficult, so think of ways to climb elegantly up into the carriage and alight from it without any mishaps.

The Food of Love

Just as your flowers, music, and transportation reflect the destination and ambience of your wedding in paradise, so should the food. Go for a taste of the destination when deciding on your catering options.

Depending on which part of the world your wedding is taking place, celebrate immediately after the ceremony with champagne and platters of fruit, chocolate-dipped strawberries, canapés in local style, or bite-size portions of local dishes.

Your celebration dinner should also include local dishes or specialties, and perhaps be accompanied by wines from the region. Ask to organize the menu well before the day so that the chef has plenty of time to cater for any special requirements.

Wedding cakes vary in type, style, and ingredients from country to country, partly because of the climate and the traditional availability of produce.

In some countries, such as Australia, an inedible plastic icing is used because of the hot weather. European wedding cakes can take the form of a sumptuous chocolate confection, while sponge cakes decorated and filled with fresh fruit are a favorite in some of the island destinations. Small, individually decorated cupcakes arranged at different levels make a stunning display and enable everyone to reach in and have their own individual piece of your special day.

photography & videography

Your wedding album is a permanent record of your day and something you'll be showing your children and their children in years to come. But how do you go about getting the wedding photographs and video you really want?

Your photographer is an important member of your wedding team—especially when you're marrying abroad. You should be made to feel at ease and you should get along well. It's important that you completely trust him or her on one of the most memorable days of your life.

The images captured on that day will be so important, not just to you, but to family and friends at home.

They will want to be able to share the joys of your wedding in paradise with you when you return.

Wedding photography has come a long way in recent years. The professional photographer has learned to be in tune with exactly what the client wants. And today's brides place emphasis on natural, spontaneous shots rather than the old "grin and bear it" pictures.

A real professional can make you and your new spouse look like you've just stepped off the pages of a glossy magazine, and keep you looking natural.

Speed is another consideration; no one wants to be standing around for ages with aching face muscles. A properly trained photographer can capture the spirit of the day and the emotions of the moment.

It's important that you meet the photographer before your big day. Show examples of the style you are after and discuss how that fits in with his or her approach and ability.

Remember that your photographer is not a mind reader —if you don't ask, then you can't really complain if you don't get what you want.

Make a photo list as this ensures that you get the pictures you want; with the excitement of the big day, one might slip your mind and you can't go back and rerun the event. Then you can check through your list to make sure that everything has been taken and you have some comeback if it's all been agreed on beforehand.

If your photography is part of a wedding package, make sure you find out exactly what it entails.

Chances are it won't include reprints or enlargements so it's wise to build such charges into your budget.

Consider having some additional shots taken at a nearby location that gives a feel of the destination you're marrying in. It's worth doing a little research and finding some scenic spot with local color, even if it means taking a taxi to the location. Reportage-style shots are a wonderful memento of your special day, in contrast to the more formal ones that your photographer will be taking at the ceremony.

It's worth looking for ideas on websites and in magazines to see what is achievable and making up your own storyboard to show your photographer.

There are things that you just won't notice on the day and funny happenings that go on behind the scenes—things you would want to see or be part of if you weren't otherwise engaged. The best way to relive your wedding day is with a wedding video.

Arrange to meet your videographer before your big day and provide a detailed brief of what you want and how you want it presented. If possible, ask to see some examples of his or her work to check the quality and style. Check whether the person you are chatting to will be doing the filming.

Find out exactly what is included in the price and if there are any extra charges for editing, adding titles, or dubbing music. Ask if you can choose your own music.

You also need to know how many copies of the video you will receive, and what the charges are for extra copies. Do ask if the videographer will carry a backup video camera, in case of equipment failure.

Don't forget to ask if your wedding will be captured on CD, DVD, or VHS tape, and check which format you will be given. This is especially important in some countries where technology isn't always compatible with that at home.

gifts

Weddings abroad often solve the dilemma of what to buy the couple who has everything. So if you're sending out a gift list, why not include some personal items that will add a touch of luxury as well as be useful on your trip of a lifetime?

For both bride and groom, silk robes are a decadent option.

Include some smaller items on both your lists for individual gifts from younger relatives and children. His and her beach towels, a manicure set, a credit card holder, and a good travel guide to the area you'll be staying in are just a few suggestions.

And if you really want to look and feel like a celebrity, why not add designer sunglasses to your list?

Some guests will want to buy traditional wedding gifts and bring them to your post-nuptial party when you return home. So you will also need to have the usual gift list.

When listing gifts that you would like to receive, include make, color, and price, and try to consider all your guests by incorporating items in different price ranges.

A set of designer luggage is an ideal present. This can include suitcases, a duffel bag, cosmetic case for the bride, and a carryon bag. You can continue the matching theme with passport holders, checkbook holders, wallets, and even luxury toiletry bags.

You will want to capture every single moment of your special day.

Why not have a camera or camcorder on your list, plus a leather-bound portfolio and stylish gilt-edged book to use as a journal to record details of your time in paradise? A good-quality pen for signing the register is also a very acceptable gift and will be a lasting keepsake of that special moment.

For him, a shaving kit in a leather case is a useful item as are cufflinks. For her, a leather jewelry case in a soft delicate shade and a powder compact, which can be engraved, are great luxury items.

DESTINATION GIFT CHECKLIST

- [ ] Large suitcase
- [ ] Medium suitcase
- [ ] Small suitcase
- [ ] Travel tote
- [ ] Carryon bag
- [ ] Cosmetic case
- [ ] Passport holders

- [ ] Checkbook holder
- [ ] Wallet
- [ ] Purse/wallet
- [ ] Credit card holder
- [ ] His and hers toiletry bags
- [ ] Gilt-edged journal

- [ ] Fountain pen
- [ ] Digital camera
- [ ] Camcorder
- [ ] Matching silk robes
- [ ] Beach towels
- [ ] Designer sunglasses
- [ ] Travel guide

For Him
- [ ] Cufflinks
- [ ] Travel shaving kit

For Her
- [ ] Jewelry bag or roll
- [ ] Powder compact
- [ ] Manicure set

WEDDING GIFT CHECKLIST

This list is intended to be used as a guide to selecting items for your wedding gift list and may not include every gift idea.

Tableware (Formal/Casual)
- [ ] Accent plates
- [ ] Butter dish
- [ ] Cereal bowls
- [ ] China, 6-piece place settings
- [ ] Coffeepot
- [ ] Creamer
- [ ] Cups and saucers
- [ ] Dessert dishes
- [ ] Gravy boat
- [ ] Mugs
- [ ] Oven-to-table ware
- [ ] Soup bowls
- [ ] Soup tureen
- [ ] Sugar bowl
- [ ] Teapot

Flatware
- [ ] Butter knife
- [ ] Cake knife
- [ ] Cake server
- [ ] Carving knife set
- [ ] Cheese knife
- [ ] Fish knives and forks

- [ ] Flatware, 6-piece settings
- [ ] Placemats/napkins
- [ ] Serving spoons
- [ ] Steak knives

Glassware
- [ ] Beer tankards
- [ ] Brandy glasses
- [ ] Champagne flutes
- [ ] Decanter
- [ ] Liqueur glasses
- [ ] Red wine glasses
- [ ] White wine glasses
- [ ] Water pitcher
- [ ] Tumblers

Kitchenware
- [ ] Baking pans
- [ ] Blender
- [ ] Bread knife
- [ ] Can opener
- [ ] Casserole dishes
- [ ] Cheese board
- [ ] Deep frier
- [ ] Electric carving knife

- [ ] Food processor
- [ ] Frying pan
- [ ] Garlic press
- [ ] Iron
- [ ] Ironing board
- [ ] Kitchen knives
- [ ] Knife sharpener
- [ ] Microwave
- [ ] Mixer
- [ ] Mixing bowls
- [ ] Quiche dish
- [ ] Salad bowl and servers
- [ ] Salt and pepper mills
- [ ] Sandwich toaster
- [ ] Saucepan set
- [ ] Soufflé dish
- [ ] Spice rack
- [ ] Storage jars
- [ ] Kettle
- [ ] Tea towels
- [ ] Toaster oven
- [ ] Trays
- [ ] Waffle iron
- [ ] Wok

Linens and Home Accessories
- [ ] Bathroom scale
- [ ] Bath rugs
- [ ] Bedspread
- [ ] Blankets
- [ ] Candleholders
- [ ] Clock
- [ ] Cushions
- [ ] Down comforter
- [ ] DVD player/recorder
- [ ] Electric blanket
- [ ] Fruit bowl
- [ ] Lamps
- [ ] Pillows
- [ ] Quilt
- [ ] Radio
- [ ] Sheet sets
- [ ] Table linen
- [ ] Towels
- [ ] TV
- [ ] Vacuum cleaner
- [ ] Wine cooler
- [ ] Wine rack

the ceremony

It's easy to be swept away by the thought of holding your ceremony on faraway shores. If you do choose a popular exotic destination, be aware that you might not be the only couple exchanging your vows under a palm tree.

Before choosing your hotel, check on the number of weddings it carries out in one day. Some resorts stage so many that newlyweds can find themselves sharing their special day with a lot more people than they intended.

If you want a secluded romantic atmosphere for your ceremony, shop around and choose a tailor-made package to avoid being a production-line bride.

Is It Legal?

This is an important question and one that all couples should ask when thinking of getting married in another country.

You can check the legalities with your wedding coordinator, and the embassy or consulate of the country in which you are to be married, but to be doubly sure, make your own legal checks with a lawyer. This may seem unnecessary now, but in later years if the legality of your marriage is called into question, it will have been worthwhile.

In some destinations it's usual for overseas authorities to finalize the paperwork after the wedding. Your original marriage certificate may be retained for this purpose, which can take some time to complete. The final documentation will be forwarded to you once the details have been completed.

Marriages solemnized abroad, in accordance with the laws of a foreign country, can't always be registered in your home country. However, in some cases, a record can be kept at an official government department. For details of this check with the appropriate office in your town or city.

First Steps

Although you've handled some of the legalities before leaving home and made a note of any special touches you want at your ceremony, your main planning will take place at your first face-to-face meeting with the hotel's wedding coordinator soon after you arrive.

Make sure you are well prepared for this meeting and jot down any questions you want to ask about any of the services provided.

Take with you sketches or pictures of the style of any items you particularly want provided at the ceremony.

If you're not sure about any of the arrangements or want to change anything, this is the time to say so—it's no good waiting until the morning of the ceremony.

In tropical and warmer climates weddings tend to take place in the late afternoon, which is the coolest part of the day. Ask for a schedule for the day and book hair and beauty appointments at the spa or salon. It's also advisable to arrange a meeting with the photographer to discuss exactly what you want.

Before the wedding you may have to go to the nearest town or city to obtain your marriage license. Check that you have all the legal documents required and allow plenty of time for this procedure. In some cases the coordinator will accompany you to lend a helping hand. If not, and you feel apprehensive, ask if a member of staff is available to go with you, particularly where there are language difficulties.

Your Special Day

On your wedding morning have a leisurely breakfast, and perhaps take a dip in the ocean or pool to revive and relax.

Book into the spa for a relaxing treatment before having a light lunch. Do drink plenty of water and juices during the day, otherwise you will dehydrate. This combined with pre-wedding nerves may result in your feeling light-headed or even fainting.

After lunch take a long leisurely bath or shower, and relax for an hour. At the hottest point of the day you need to be inside your room to stay cool. Then visit the salon for your hair to be styled. If you're having a makeup artist, it's better that they come to your room or suite to complete this. The motto for the day is "don't rush—take your time" in order to avoid looking and feeling hot and bothered.

The celebrant conducting your service will meet with you either prior to the day or just before the wedding. Make him or her aware of any special points you want mentioned, and if you have a reading or poem to be included, provide a clear printed copy.

When it's time to make your way to your wedding location, your coordinator will be there to take care of all the arrangements, making sure everything runs smoothly.

The ceremony will involve readings and usually a short address by the celebrant, as well as the legal formalities required by law.

If you don't have any witnesses, these can be provided for you by the coordinator.

After the formalities there's time for photographs and you may wish to ask your celebrant, coordinator, and any guests you have met during your stay to join you for champagne and canapés to toast your married life.

Whether it's on a tropical island, in a fairytale castle, or in the gardens of some idyllic luxury hotel, as the sun sets on the first evening of your married life together, it will create feelings that will last a lifetime.

after the wedding

The trip of a lifetime is over and it's time for you to return home to share the joy and happiness of your special day with your friends and family. You may have already arranged a post-nuptial party to celebrate your marriage. In which case, let the festivities commence!

Before the official post-nuptial celebration it's a nice idea to hold a dinner party for both sets of parents. Your new home is the ideal venue—here they can watch the video and share the events of your special day in intimate surroundings. It's bound to be an emotional occasion and they will be able to shed a tear or two in the privacy of your home as they watch their children make their solemn vows and embark on the first moments of their new life together.

If a dinner party in your new home is impracticable or you live a distance away, visit each set of parents, take champagne and canapés and watch the video before taking them out to dine at their favorite hotel or restaurant.

In the days before your party you may want to officially announce your marriage. There are two ways of doing this. You can put an announcement in the newspaper, stating when and where the wedding took place, or opt for an announcement card.

Cards are a good way of letting everyone know you are now Mr. and Mrs.—especially if you've tied the knot without telling anyone. The cards can be printed before your wedding so they are ready to mail out on your return. The wording inside should be simple and could read something like this:

Jane Alice Doe
and
John David Brown
are happy to announce their marriage
on Thursday the seventh of June
Ashford Castle, County Mayo, Ireland

You may want to add your new address and contact details as well, or a handwritten message to personalize the announcement.

The Post-nuptial Party

Your party can be exactly what you want it to be—from a formal reception for a large number of guests to an informal gathering of family, friends, and colleagues. The location can be flexible too. If it's in the summer months why not go for a garden party for your celebratory meal?

As with all weddings it's important that the room and surroundings are appropriately decorated. You can either opt for traditional wedding decor and table decorations, or be brave and theme your room. If your marriage took place in an island paradise setting, go for a bright color scheme. Decorate your tables with tropical flowers and serve cocktails as an aperitif. You can set the scene with mood music of the islands, or even take it further and hire a steel band or calypso singer.

The format of the party is again open to choice. Some couples choose the traditional reception-style pattern. Guests assemble for pre-dinner drinks after which they are greeted by the parents of the bride and groom as they enter the dining room. The newlyweds then make their entrance when everyone is seated.

Others opt for a more dramatic approach, arriving at the venue in the transportation of their choice. With the guests already assembled in the function room, they make a grand entrance to the center or head of the room where they can repeat their vows in front of their guests and receive a blessing if they so wish. Couples who want a more private atmosphere for this very personal act of commitment can make arrangements for their close family and friends to attend a service of blessing at a local church immediately before the post-nuptial reception.

Speeches are not compulsory at your party, but odds are that the bride's father and some other members of the family will want to say a few words to commemorate such a special occasion. Then after the obligatory cake-cutting and champagne toasts there's only one thing left to do—dance the night away and enjoy.

Obviously you'll want to show off your photographs so think carefully about how you're going to display them. Get some professional help with making your "wedding exhibition." Extra lighting, handwritten captions, decorated boards, or poetic quotations will add to the attractiveness of the display. You could consider having a collage made of souvenirs including airline tickets, brochures, menus from the hotel, pressed flowers from your bouquet, some reportage-style informal photographs, champagne corks, a piece of fabric from your dress, and other reminders of your destination.

Naturally everyone will want to watch the video of your ceremony so do make sure the venue you've chosen has a big screen and a sound system, or is able to hire in the necessary equipment. If your gathering is a large one, it may be necessary to have more than one screen so that all the guests have a clear view of the video.

What you wear for this occasion is a personal choice. You may both want to wear the dress and outfit you had for your wedding ceremony or, if you were married in informal outfits, you might like to choose a special gown in a traditional style and a tuxedo for this occasion.

countdown to the big day

One of the secrets of planning a successful and stress-free wedding is to be well organized. With this month-by-month guide you can see what preparations are needed prior to jetting off to the day of your dreams. Just follow the plan, checking off each step in order to ensure that nothing is forgotten or left to chance.

12–6 months before

- [ ] Decide together on a destination. Be prepared to compromise and research various options. Contact tourist offices for brochures and any other information you may need.

- [ ] Contact the embassy or consulate of the country where you are to be married to establish the legalities and residency period for foreigners. Ascertain exactly what documents are required and whether any need to be translated.

- [ ] Consult a lawyer to make sure of any legalities affecting your marriage abroad.

- [ ] Tell both sets of parents the news that you have decided to tie the knot in an overseas destination. Arrange a break-the-ice lunch or dinner even if they've already met.

- [ ] Book your flights, hotel accommodations, or all-inclusive wedding package with your travel agent or tour operator well in advance, especially if your chosen date falls on or near a major holiday either at home or in your wedding destination. Confirm that the airline is notified that you're traveling with your wedding dress when your reservations are made.

- [ ] Inform any close friends, family, or relatives who are accompanying you of the exact date of your departure and wedding, and book their accommodations and flights with your travel agent.

- [ ] Organize your passports and any visas that are required. Note that new passports can take several weeks to arrive. Check if there are requirements for blank pages in your passport. Also check that it has at least six months before expiry by the time you return home (these regulations can change quickly so re-check before you travel).

- [ ] Remind the rest of the wedding party to check passports and to apply for any necessary visas.

- [ ] Take out travel insurance.

- [ ] If opting to make arrangements for your wedding independently with the hotel, contact the onsite wedding coordinator to book the ceremony and ascertain what the legal requirements are. Inform the coordinator of your requirements and ask for a list of services/ suppliers that are available.

- [ ] Start to look for a gown for yourself and, if you're having bridesmaids, their dresses too. If you're having your outfits made to order, make an appointment with your designer.

- [ ] Decide on the groom's and bestman's attire.

- [ ] If you're having a party to celebrate when you return home, look for a suitable venue and make a firm booking. Organize caterers, entertainment, or furniture rental if required.

4 months

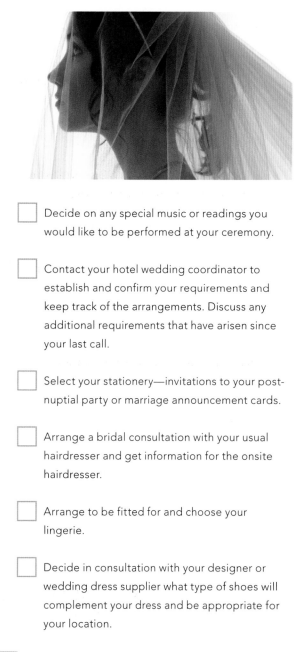

☐ Decide on any special music or readings you would like to be performed at your ceremony.

☐ Contact your hotel wedding coordinator to establish and confirm your requirements and keep track of the arrangements. Discuss any additional requirements that have arisen since your last call.

☐ Select your stationery—invitations to your post-nuptial party or marriage announcement cards.

☐ Arrange a bridal consultation with your usual hairdresser and get information for the onsite hairdresser.

☐ Arrange to be fitted for and choose your lingerie.

☐ Decide in consultation with your designer or wedding dress supplier what type of shoes will complement your dress and be appropriate for your location.

3 months

☐ Check with your doctor whether you will need any vaccinations or if you need a course of malaria pills. Make an appointment for a pre-wedding health check.

☐ Visit your dentist for pre-wedding checks.

☐ If your flight is an early one, reserve a room at an airport hotel to ensure a smooth getaway.

☐ Start shopping for your honeymoon wardrobe.

☐ Arrange a meeting with your beauty therapist to discuss your requirements.

☐ Have a consultation with a makeup artist and ask for advice on products that are best suited to the climate in which you're marrying.

☐ Visit your favorite beauty counter and purchase makeup and skincare products, as your usual brands and favorite colors may not be available in the destination of your choice.

☐ Book hair appointments up to and including the day before you travel.

2 months

- ☐ Liaise with your hotel wedding coordinator to check arrangements.

- ☐ Book transportation or taxis to the airport, or arrange airport parking.

- ☐ Send out invitations to your post-nuptial party, including your gift list.

- ☐ Contact local hotels to arrange accommodations for guests at your post-wedding party, and transportation for guests who require it.

1 month

- ☐ Review your wardrobe and luggage needs.

- ☐ Check with your airline about baggage allowance and the arrangements for transporting your wedding dress. Certain airlines will supply dress bags while others store the dress separately on board.

- ☐ Finalize the guest list for your post-nuptial party and confirm the numbers with the venue.

- ☐ Arrange a trial run for your hair and makeup.

- ☐ Book beauty treatments and manicures for just before your departure.

- ☐ Arrange bachelor and bachelorette parties.

- ☐ Order your currency and traveler's checks.

- ☐ Check that your wedding outfits will be ready in time.

1 week

☐ Check that friends and family traveling to your destination have all the relevant documentation organized.

☐ Have your trial run for your hair and makeup, and wear your wedding shoes at home.

☐ Pack and confirm reservations with airlines and travel agents.

☐ Arrange a pre-nuptial dinner for your close friends and family.

2 days to go

☐ Celebrate your pre-nuptial dinner with your close friends and family.

the day before your departure

☐ Make a point of visiting your parents to say au revoir if they're not going with you, and leave them your itinerary and contact details, including phone numbers, email addresses, and the time of your return flight.

☐ Check outward flight times, and airport hotel accommodations.

… Bon voyage and good luck!

destination checklist

- [ ] passports/visas
- [ ] birth certificates
- [ ] international driving license
- [ ] currency/traveler's checks
- [ ] travel insurance documents
- [ ] hotel reservation documents
- [ ] plane tickets
- [ ] car reservation documents
- [ ] other documentation (if necessary)
- [ ] medication
- [ ] wedding vows
- [ ] wedding itinerary
- [ ] wedding coordinator's contact details
- [ ] wedding outfits
- [ ] headdress
- [ ] shoes
- [ ] the rings
- [ ] gifts

- [ ] music (if bringing your own)
- [ ] swimwear
- [ ] evening wear
- [ ] casual daywear
- [ ] jewelry
- [ ] undergarments
- [ ] camera
- [ ] cell phone
- [ ] address book
- [ ] insect repellent
- [ ] guidebook
- [ ] makeup
- [ ] hair accessories
- [ ] toiletries
- [ ] perfume
- [ ] wet weather clothes (if necessary)
- [ ] warm clothes (if necessary)
- [ ] sun protection

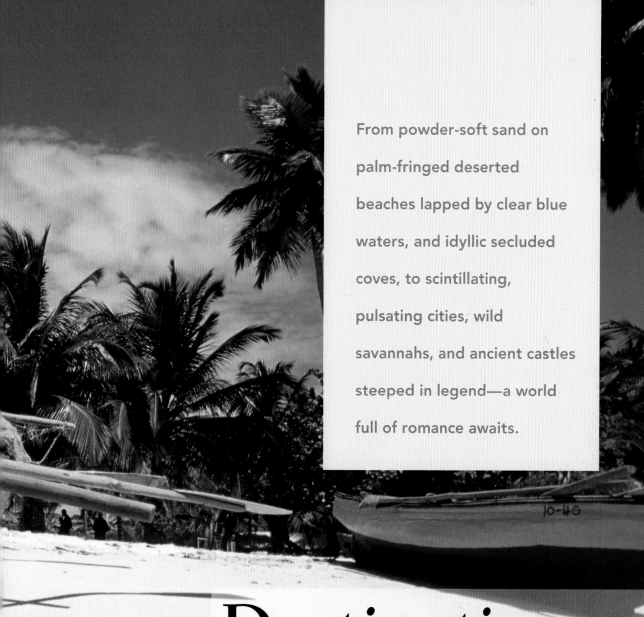

From powder-soft sand on
palm-fringed deserted
beaches lapped by clear blue
waters, and idyllic secluded
coves, to scintillating,
pulsating cities, wild
savannahs, and ancient castles
steeped in legend—a world
full of romance awaits.

Destinations

Locator Map

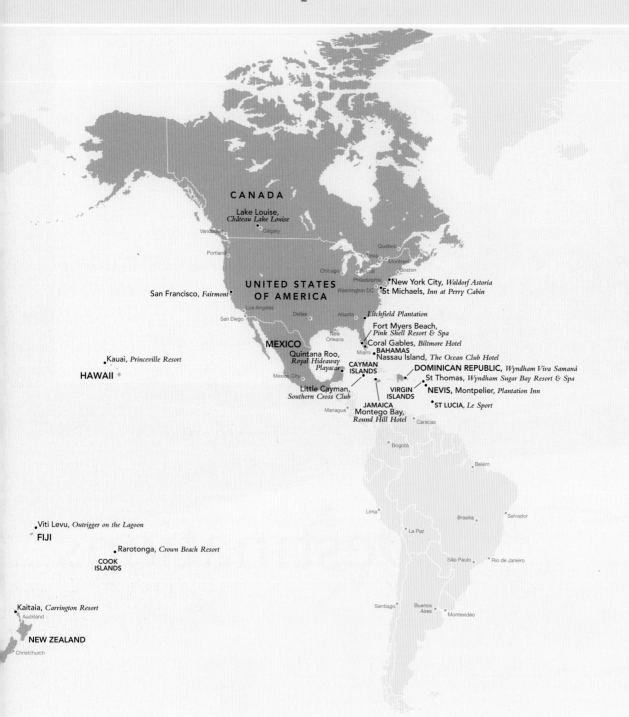

CANADA

Lake Louise,
Château Lake Louise

Vancouver •   • Calgary

Portland •

Québec •

Ottawa •   • Montreal

Chicago •   • Detroit   • Boston

**UNITED STATES
OF AMERICA**

Philadelphia •

Washington DC •

• **New York City,** *Waldorf Astoria*

• **St Michaels,** *Inn at Perry Cabin*

San Francisco, *Fairmont* •

Los Angeles •

San Diego •

Dallas •

Atlanta •

• *Litchfield Plantation*

Fort Myers Beach,
Pink Shell Resort & Spa

New
Orleans

• **Coral Gables,** *Biltmore Hotel*

MEXICO

Miami •   **BAHAMAS**
   • **Nassau Island,** *The Ocean Club Hotel*

Quintana Roo,
*Royal Hideaway
Playacar*

**CAYMAN
ISLANDS**

DOMINICAN REPUBLIC, *Wyndham Viva Samaná*

• **St Thomas,** *Wyndham Sugar Bay Resort & Spa*

Kauai, *Princeville Resort* •

HAWAII •

Mexico City •

Little Cayman,
Southern Cross Club

**VIRGIN
ISLANDS**

• **NEVIS,** Montpelier, *Plantation Inn*

• **ST LUCIA,** *Le Sport*

JAMAICA
Montego Bay,
Round Hill Hotel

Managua •

Caracas •

Bogotá •

Belém •

• Viti Levu, *Outrigger on the Lagoon*

FIJI

Lima •

Brasília •

Salvador •

• Rarotonga, *Crown Beach Resort*

**COOK
ISLANDS**

La Paz •

São Paulo •   • Rio de Janeiro

Kaitaia, *Carrington Resort* •

Auckland •

Santiago •

Buenos
Aires •   • Montevideo

NEW ZEALAND

Christchurch •

Jukkasjärvi, *Icehotel*

SWEDEN

FINLAND

Helsinki, *Kämp Hotel*

Oslo
Stockholm
St Petersburg
Moscow
Novosibirsk
Irkutsk

UNITED
KINGDOM

Kilchrenan, *Ardanaseig Hotel*
County Mayo, *Ashford Castle*
IRELAND
Dublin
Oxford,
Le Manoir aux Quat'Saisons
Berlin
Jersey,
Longueville Manor
London
Paris
FRANCE
Venice,
Hotel Cipriani
Côte d'Azur,
*Château de la
Chèvre d'Or*
ITALY
Rome
Lisbon
GREECE
Tunis
Algiers
Santorini,
Katikies Hotel
CYPRUS
Istanbul
Cassablanca
Kouklia,
Aphrodite Hills Resort
Tripoli
Cairo
Baghdad
Tehran
Kuwait
Jeddah

Ulaanbaatar
Tashkent
Rostov
Lahore
Delhi
Beijing
Seoul
Tokyo
Shanghai
T'ai-pei

Calcutta
Hong Kong
Mombai
Hanoi
Manila
THAILAND
Madras
Bangkok
Ho Chi Minh
Colombo
Phuket, *Sheraton Grand Laguna*
Kuala Lumpur
Singapore

Khartoum
Addis Ababa
Lagos

KENYA
Nairobi
Malindi,
*Hemingways
Resort*
SEYCHELLES
Silhouette Island,
Labriz Silhouette
Kinshasa
Dar es Salaam
Luanda

Harare
MAURITIUS
Belle Mare, *Le Saint Geran*
Wolmar, *Taj Exotica Resort & Spa*

AUSTRALIA
Perth

S Stradbroke Island,
*Couran Cove
Island Resort*
Bnsbane
Lord Howe Island,
Arajilla Retreat

Johannesburg
SOUTH
AFRICA
Durban
Cape Town, *The Mount Nelson Hotel*

Adelaide
Melbourne
Sydney,
Observatory Hotel
Kaitaia,
Carrington Resort
Auckland
NEW ZEALAND
Hobart
Christchurch

Bridal Files

	PAGES	WEDDING COORDINATOR	WEDDING PACKAGE	CEREMONY CONDUCTED BY*	TRANSPORTATION	MUSIC	SPA
AFRICA							
HEMINGWAYS RESORT, MALINDI, KENYA	60	●	●	R	●	●	●
MOUNT NELSON HOTEL, CAPE TOWN, SOUTH AFRICA	64	●	●	NM	●	●	●
AUSTRALIA							
ARAJILLA RETREAT, LORD HOWE ISLAND, NEW SOUTH WALES	70			C			●
THE OBSERVATORY HOTEL, SYDNEY, NEW SOUTH WALES	76	●	●	C		●	●
COURAN COVE ISLAND RESORT, SOUTH STRADBROKE ISLAND	80	●	●	C		●	●
EUROPE							
LE MANOIR AUX QUAT' SAISONS, OXFORD, ENGLAND	86	●		R		●	
HOTEL KÄMP, HELSINKI, FINLAND	92		●	LO, M		●	●
CHÂTEAU DE LA CHÈVRE D'OR, FRENCH RIVIERA, FRANCE	96			M, R		●	
ASHFORD CASTLE, COUNTY MAYO, IRELAND	100	●		P	●	●	●
HOTEL CIPRIANI, VENICE, ITALY	104			RO		●	●
ARDANAISEIG HOTEL, KILCHRENAN, SCOTLAND	110	●		M, R	●	●	
ICEHOTEL, JUKKASJÄRVI, SWEDEN	114	●		P		●	
ISLANDS							
ONE&ONLY OCEAN CLUB, PARADISE ISLAND, BAHAMAS	120	●	●	M, MO	●	●	●
SOUTHERN CROSS CLUB, LITTLE CAYMAN, CAYMAN ISLANDS	124	●	●	JP, M	●	●	●
LONGUEVILLE MANOR, JERSEY, CHANNEL ISLANDS	128	●	●	R	●	●	
CROWN BEACH RESORT, RAROTONGA, COOK ISLANDS	132	●	●	JP, M	●	●	●
HOTEL KATIKIES, SANTORINI, CYCLADES ISLANDS, GREECE	138	●	●	LO	●	●	○
THE INTERCONTINENTAL APHRODITE HILLS RESORT HOTEL, CYPRUS	142	●	●	LO	●	●	●
VIVA WYNDHAM SAMANÁ, LAS TERRANAS, DOMINICAN REPUBLIC	146	●	●	J	●	●	●
OUTRIGGER ON THE LAGOON, VITI LEVU, FIJI	150	●	●	C, M	●	●	●
PRINCEVILLE RESORT, KAUAI, HAWAII	154	●	●	DM, NM	●	●	●
ROUND HILL HOTEL, MONTEGO BAY, JAMAICA	160	●		M		●	●
ONE&ONLY LE ST GÉRAN, POSTE DE FLACQ, MAURITIUS	164	●	●	CSO	●	●	●
TAJ EXOTICA RESORT & SPA, WOLMAR, MAURITIUS	168	●	●	C		●	●
MONTPELIER PLANTATION INN, MONTPELIER, NEVIS	174	●	●	M, MG, P		●	●
CARRINGTON RESORT, KAITAIA, NORTH ISLAND, NEW ZEALAND	178	●	●	C	●	●	●
LABRIZ SILHOUETTE, SILHOUETTE ISLAND, SEYCHELLES	182	●	●	R	●	●	●
LESPORT, CAP ESTATE, ST. LUCIA	186	●	●	C		●	●
SHERATON GRANDE LAGUNA, PHUKET, THAILAND	190	●	●	C, P, TM		●	●
WYNDHAM SUGAR BAY RESORT & SPA, ST. THOMAS, U.S.V.I.	194	●	●	NM	●	●	●
THE AMERICAS							
THE FAIRMONT CHATEAU LAKE LOUISE, THE ROCKIES, CANADA	200	●	●	C, M	●	●	●
ROYAL HIDEAWAY PLAYACAR, QUINTANA ROO, MEXICO	206	●	●	JP	●	●	●
BILTMORE, MIAMI, FLORIDA	210	●		M, LO	●	●	●
PINK SHELL BEACH RESORT & SPA, FORT MYERS, FLORIDA	214	●	●	LO	●	●	●
THE INN AT PERRY CABIN, ST. MICHAELS, MARYLAND	220	●		LO	●	●	●
THE WALDORF-ASTORIA, NEW YORK	224	●		LO	●	●	●
THE FAIRMONT, SAN FRANCISCO, CALIFORNIA	228	●		LO	●	●	●
LITCHFIELD PLANTATION, PAWLEYS ISLAND, SOUTH CAROLINA	232	●	●	M, MO	●	●	●

● onsite facilities   ○ can be arranged with external suppliers by the hotel/resort

GYM	HAIR STYLIST/SALON	BEAUTY THERAPIST/SALON	MANICURIST	MASSEUR	MAKEUP ARTIST	PHOTOGRAPHER	VIDEOGRAPHER	INDIVIDUAL CAKE MADE	FLOWERS	BOUTONNIERES	FLORAL TABLE DECORATIONS	ROOM ON WEDDING DAY	VALET SERVICE

* C = celebrant; CSO = civil status officer; DM = denominational minister; J = judge; JP = justice of the peace;
LO = licensed officiant; M = minister; MG = magistrate; MO = marriage officer; NM = nondenominational minister;
P = priest; R = registrar; RO = religious officiant; TM = Thai monk

weather to travel

If you don't want to get hit by hurricanes, saturated by storms, or be frozen and frostbitten on the day of your dreams, it's wise to check the best times to travel to your destination. Winters in Europe, some parts of the U.S.A., and Canada can be very cold and, as well as being uncomfortable, the inclement weather conditions can delay and upset your travel plans. In tropical climes avoid the rainy and hurricane seasons as these can literally make your big day a washout and cause havoc with transportation and flights. High humidity and excessive heat can also cause problems and may affect you or cause you to feel unwell. Remember when traveling to places such as Australia and New Zealand that the seasons are reversed. June, July, and August are the winter months in that part of the world.

Bahamas
Temperature Range: 79°F to 90°F
Best Time: December to March
Caution: May to October wettest months. July to November possibility of hurricanes

British Isles
Temperature Range: 28°F to 79°F
Best Time: May to September
Caution: November to February winter. Weather unpredictable all year round

Canadian Rockies
Temperature Range: 32°F to 73°F
Best Time: February to March
Caution: January very cold

Cape Town
Temperature Range: 63°F to 79°F
Best Time: June to March
Caution: April and May tend to be rainy

Cayman Islands
Temperature Range: 84°F to 90°F
Best Time: November to May
Caution: June to October chance of tropical storms

Channel Islands
Temperature Range: 41°F to 75°F
Best Time: March to October
Caution: December and January cool but rarely cold

Cook Islands
Temperature Range: 64°F to 84°F
Best Time: December to May
Caution: November to April rainy season

Cyclades Islands, Greece
Temperature Range: 57°F to 90°F
Best Time: May to September
Caution: Winter high rainfall

Cyprus
Temperature Range: 43°F to 99°F
Best Time: May to November
Caution: December to April high rainfall, tends to be chilly

Dominican Republic
Temperature Range: 66°F to 88°F
Best Time: December to April
Caution: May to November rainy season, possibility of hurricanes

Fiji
Temperature Range: 84°F to 90°F
Best Time: December to May
Caution: November to April rainfall and humidity at their highest

Finland
Temperature Range: 27°F to 72°F
Best Time: May to October
Caution: November to March extremely cold

Florida
Temperature Range: 57°F to 91°F
Best Time: December to May
Caution: July to October coast prone to hurricanes

French Riviera
Temperature Range: 39°F to 81°F
Best Time: All year round

Hawaii
Temperature Range: 66°F to 86°F
Best Time: April to November
Caution: December to March rainy season

Jamaica

Temperature Range: 88°F to 93°F

Best Time: December to April

Caution: May to November heat intense with heavy tropical showers. June to November is hurricane season

Kenya

Temperature Range: 84°F to 93°F

Best Time: June to March

Caution: April and May rainy season

Lord Howe Island

Temperature Range: 52°F to 84°F

Best Time: April to October

Caution: November to March monsoon rains, torrential downpours, high humidity

Maryland

Temperature Range: 36°F to 88°F

Best Time: May to October

Caution: November to March winter season

Mauritius

Temperature Range: 75°F to 84°F

Best Time: May to November

Caution: December to April rainy season

Mexico

Temperature Range: 86°F to 97°F

Best Time: November, January to March

Caution: June and July excessively hot, tropical storms; April and May, September to December periods of high rainfall. June to November is hurricane season

Nevis

Temperature Range: 81°F to 86°F

Best Time: February to April

Caution: July to November rainy season, possibility of hurricanes

New York

Temperature Range: 27°F to 82°F

Best Time: April to September

Caution: November to March can be bitterly cold with severe weather conditions

New Zealand

Temperature Range: 43°F to 73°F

Best Time: October to March

Caution: June to August winter

Phuket, Thailand

Temperature Range: 88°F to 93°F

Best Time: November to May

Caution: June to October rainy season

St. Lucia

Temperature Range: 82°F to 88°F

Best Time: December to May

Caution: June to November hurricane season with tropical storms, heavy rainfall

San Francisco

Temperature Range: 41°F to 73°F

Best Time: April to September

Caution: October to March winter, likely to rain

Seychelles

Temperature Range: 82°F to 88°F

Best Time: October to April

Caution: November to March increase in rainfall, trade winds bring seaweed to some beaches

South Carolina

Temperature Range: 36°F to 88°F

Best Time: April to September

Caution: December to May unpredictable weather, with hurricane season from June to November

South Stradbroke Island

Temperature Range: 52°F to 84°F

Best Time: April to October

Caution: November to March monsoon rains, torrential downpours, high humidity

Sweden

Temperature Range: 5°F to 77°F

Best Time: May to September

Caution: December to March can be very cold

Sydney

Temperature Range: 46°F to 79°F

Best Time: February to November

Caution: December and January hottest months

U.S. Virgin Islands

Temperature Range: 77°F to 82°F

Best Time: January to April

Caution: July to November rainy season, tropical storms, possibility of hurricanes

Venice

Temperature Range: 34°F to 81°F

Best Time: April to September

Caution: October to March can be very gloomy

Dramatic scenery, snow-capped mountains, golden beaches, vibrant cities, and vast swathes of savannah where nature reigns supreme. Take a walk on the wild side, and experience Africa—a continent of amazing contrasts.

Africa

hemingways resort
MALINDI
KENYA

"a sophisticated, secluded haven"

From sundrenched beaches lined with swaying coconut palms bordering on the crystal clear waters of the Indian Ocean to spectacular game parks with their vast and beautiful terrain, Kenya is an exciting wedding and honeymoon destination. Watch the sunset over the rippling waters of the ocean fanned by the cool breeze, or skim silently over the savannah in a hot-air balloon. Walk on the wild side and stay in a luxury game lodge, or go on safari the way it should be, sleeping under canvas beneath the stars.

Kenya is a country of contrasts like no other. It's a place of breathtaking snow-capped mountains, warm blue seas and vast swathes of savannah where nature reigns supreme and extreme.

The grasslands of East Africa offer the most famous wildlife spectacle in the world, and nowhere else is there such a wide and stunning variety of wildlife so easily observed.

BELOW
Bird's-eye view of the resort.

Where else can you see a family of hippos basking in the river or a lioness nursing her cubs under the shade of an akubia tree, or in the cool of the evening watch animals gathering around the watering holes? Add to this the excitement of seeing the famed Big Five—elephant, rhino, lion, leopard, and buffalo—roam the reserves together with hundreds of other species, and you'll understand the magic that is Kenya.

Meanwhile, Kenya's tropical coast boasts over 300 miles of beaches lapped by the Indian Ocean—so combine a stay in both environments and you have the ingredients for the perfect wedding and honeymoon.

Sixty miles north of Mombasa and 12 miles south of Malindi Airport is one of the best beach hotels on the Indian Ocean. Perched on the quiet Watamu Beach is Hemingways, a sophisticated, secluded haven.

An oceanfront swimming pool sparkles under the palms. The white sand beach, which is second to none, stretches for as far as the eye can see, and the waters within the reef are broken up by huge coral outcrops.

Hemingways has a wonderfully relaxed atmosphere. Its 74 rooms and suites are decorated in colonial style with private bathrooms, air-conditioning, ceiling fans, and mosquito nets. Some of the suites have enclosed patios, while all have large queen-size beds.

The hotel is renowned for its leisure facilities, particularly deep-sea fishing, scuba diving, waterskiing, windsurfing, and snorkeling in Watamu Marine Park.

ABOVE
Hemingways overlooks the beautiful beach of Watamu Marine Park.

—

RIGHT AND BOTTOM RIGHT
An Executive Suite and a Junior Suite at the resort. All suites have ocean views.

VITAL STATISTICS

rooms 74 rooms/suites

email reservations@
hemingways.co.ke

website
www.hemingways.co.ke

legal requirements

- Minimum residence in
  Kenya 5 days before
  ceremony. No weddings
  take place in Kenya from
  December 22 to January 6
- To marry in Kenya you
  will need to apply for
  a special license
- Two witnesses are
  required

documents required

- Ten-year valid passport
- Birth certificate
- A valid Kenyan tourist
  permit, obtained in
  advance
- The legalities are
  complex, so it's
  recommended that
  you contact the Kenyan
  Embassy or Consulate
  in your own city or state
  for full information on
  the documents required,
  and legal procedures for
  marrying in Kenya

Facilities on land include a gym, two idyllically landscaped swimming pools, and a lively bar.

The thatched-roof restaurant is renowned for its high standard of cuisine and service, or you can dine under the stars by candlelight for a truly romantic experience.

Weddings at Hemingways are highly romantic. The resort has a wedding package and an onsite wedding coordinator to take care of all the details.

Couples can tie the knot in the tropical garden with a choice of beach or ocean background. An exciting option for a unique wedding, or wedding and reception setting, is on board an Arab wooden dhow under sail, subject to availability and weather conditions.

Marriages are conducted by the registrar and an unusual optional extra is to have a Swahili church choir sing at your ceremony.

Afterwards the couple can savor a private dinner under the romantic African starlit sky before returning to their flower-filled room where a bottle of chilled wine awaits.

BRIDAL FILE

- *Onsite wedding coordinator*
- *Wedding package*
- *Weddings take place on beach, in garden, or on board traditional Arab dhow*
- *Ceremony conducted by registrar*
- *Transportation: vintage cars & limousines*
- *Music: Swahili church choir*
- *Mini spa*
- *Photographer & videographer*
- *Wedding cake*
- *Bridal bouquet & boutonnieres*

TOP LEFT

The oceanfront pool sparkles under the palms.

—

BOTTOM

Preparing for a candlelight dinner on the terrace.

Hemingways is the perfect place to use as a base for a safari throughout Kenya. These are varied and bookable onsite in order to take advantage of up-to-date weather conditions and game movements.

But if you want to spend the whole of your trip at Hemingways there are plenty of adventures on offer. Take a trip in a glassbottom boat, cruise through the mangrove forests in a dhow, or just chill out with a cold drink and watch the magical African sunset.

LEFT

Take a dhow cruise on Mida Creek—a sanctuary for exotic birdlife.

mount nelson hotel
CAPE TOWN
SOUTH AFRICA

"a hot and happening destination"

Cape Town is the perfect year-round destination for exchanging your vows, from the majestic towering cliffs of Table Mountain to its sun-soaked beaches spectacularly situated between sea and mountain. Built on a peninsula, where the Indian and Atlantic oceans meet, it's a colorful city, with havens of tranquility amid the throbbing energy of its colonial streets. Swim, sunbathe or surf, stroll around exotic gardens, or experience the breathtaking beauty of the valleys and vineyards—the choice is yours.

South Africa is famed for its natural beauty, stunning coastline, and unrivaled game reserves. As a wedding and honeymoon destination, beach and bushland are what immediately spring to mind. But it has much more to offer.

Cape Town is one of South Africa's incredible cities. It's unique, fascinating, and a hot and happening destination buzzing with a rich culture and spirit found in few other places.

Within an easy stroll of the city center, lies Cape Town's most famous hotel—the Mount Nelson. Set amid glorious gardens at the foot of Table Mountain, the beautiful blush of the hotel's pale pink exterior is unmistakable.

For over a century its style, impeccable service, and celebrity guests have given this award-winning hotel its worldwide landmark status.

Since 1899 the hotel has played host to the rich and famous. Royalty, diplomats, presidents, and Hollywood VIPs have strolled its emerald lawns, dined in its opulent restaurants, and enjoyed the grace and charm of luxurious living, which the hotel still offers today.

VITAL STATISTICS

rooms 57 suites and
144 bedrooms

email reservations@
mountnelson.co.za

website
www.mountnelson.co.za

legal requirements

- Minimum age without
  parental consent 21

documents required

- Passport with at least two
  blank pages
- Birth certificate
- Divorce decree if
  divorced
- Death certificate of
  former spouse
  if widowed
- Adoption certificate
  if applicable

BOTTOM LEFT

A reception in a party tent
overlooking the gardens.

———

ABOVE

The hotel occupies a
breathtaking site on the
lower slopes of Table
Mountain.

———

RIGHT

A Garden Cottage Suite.

The Mount Nelson Hotel has
six individual wings, separated from the
main hotel, each with its own unique
character, private gardens, and facilities.
Each of the 57 suites and 144 bedrooms
is individually furnished.

The romance and decadence of the
bedrooms are reflected in their fabrics,
draped or four-poster beds, crystal
chandeliers, and marble bathrooms, all
with magnificent views over the gardens
or the legendary Table Mountain.

BRIDAL FILE

- Onsite wedding coordinator
- 2 wedding packages
- Weddings take place in the gardens
- Ceremony conducted by nondenominational minister
- Transportation: vintage cars & limousines
- Music: local musicians playing traditional music, local choir, classical/modern singer, taped music, organist/pianist, string duo/trio/quartet, harpist
- Spa, gym, hair salon
- Hair stylist, beauty therapist, manicurist, masseur, makeup artist
- Photographer & videographer
- Individually designed cake
- Flowers & boutonnieres
- Floral table decorations
- Separate room for the bride and groom to prepare for the wedding

Dining at the Mount Nelson Hotel is an unforgettable experience. The elegant Cape Colony restaurant is renowned for its fine dining. The Oasis Restaurant offers alfresco dining at its best, while the Mount Nelson's world-famous, award-winning afternoon tea, served on the veranda, terrace, or in the lounge, is an experience to be savored.

With its unique setting at the foot of Table Mountain, lush gardens, and spa of unsurpassed luxury with four of the ten rooms offering dual treatments for couples, the Mount Nelson is the perfect place to say "I do."

The hotel offers two wedding packages and has an onsite wedding coordinator.

Marriages are performed by a nondenominational minister in the glorious gardens and a backup venue is always reserved in the event of inclement weather.

After the ceremony, savor vintage champagne in the Planet bar under the African sky before a romantic dinner in the restaurant. When it's finally time to retire to your room, you'll find roses on your bed and petals in the bathtub; a basket of fruit and a bottle of chilled champagne await your pleasure.

Cape Town is a melting pot of history and culture and there are lots of places to visit: take the revolving cable car to the top of Table Mountain; escape to Boulders Beach, the one place in the world where you can swim and sunbathe with penguins; stroll along the Victoria and Alfred Waterfront with its eclectic mix of designer boutiques, craft, and coffee shops, and its plethora of ships and sailing vessels; or follow the wine routes along Cape Town's valleys.

LEFT
The grace and charm of the Mount Nelson Hotel and the Kitchener Fountain.

———

ABOVE
Enjoy quiet sophistication and style in an unmatched setting.

———

BELOW
Relax and take a dip in the two heated pools.

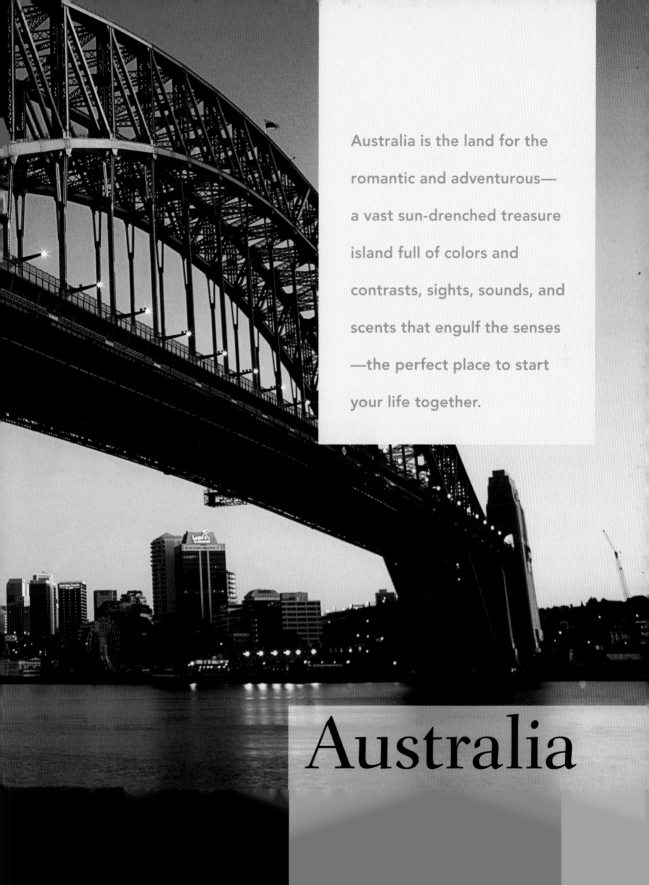

Australia is the land for the romantic and adventurous—a vast sun-drenched treasure island full of colors and contrasts, sights, sounds, and scents that engulf the senses —the perfect place to start your life together.

Australia

arajilla retreat
LORD HOWE ISLAND
NEW SOUTH WALES

"Jewel of the Pacific"

Spectacular volcanic peaks, deep rain forests, rolling surf, and turquoise lagoons—Lord Howe Island is the ultimate island paradise. Wake up to a symphony of birdsong, stroll hand in hand alongside stunning lagoons, or immerse yourself in the sound of rolling waves with a private candlelight beach dinner created especially for you. Sit in lush meadows with a gourmet picnic basket, explore the rain forests, or dive and discover the rich colorful underwater world of the island's famous lagoons.

Less than two hours' flight from Sydney and Brisbane is New South Wales's beautiful Lord Howe Island. Often referred to as the "Jewel of the Pacific," it has the unique distinction of being one of only a handful of island groups to have a World Heritage listing.

Situated in the Tasman Sea off Australia's east coast, the island is only 6 miles long and 1 mile wide at its broadest point. It has a remarkable volcanic geology and a rare collection of plants, birds, and marine life, plus an exceptional beauty. A wedding and honeymoon here will leave life-long memories of a truly magical experience.

Life on Lord Howe is unhurried. There's no mobile phone reception, bicycles are the main form of transportation, and the island's few motor vehicles are restricted to 15 mph. There are no high-rise buildings and no power lines to spoil its beautiful views.

Nestled under a canopy of Kentia palms and banyan trees just minutes from the beach is Arajilla Retreat. Idyllic and concealed, it seems made for honeymooners to share their intimate moments, and will provide a romantic experience that will long be remembered.

ABOVE

Crags and coves carve out secluded beaches in this South Pacific paradise.

RIGHT

Friendly fish at Neds Beach.

—

BELOW

The guest lounge
surrounded by timber
decks and native flora.

Pathways meander through the
forest connecting the 12 suites and
apartments, each with its own private
deck. Each features beautiful interiors
by a leading Australian interior designer,
queen-size beds, and every amenity
for your comfort.

Arajilla Retreat offers guests the
choice of dining inside or outside on the
deck in the large and open restaurant.
Lit at night by candles, it is renowned for
its creative menu.

VITAL STATISTICS

rooms 12 suites/apartments

email arajilla@lordhowe.com.au

website www.arajilla.com.au

legal requirements

- The couple must complete a certificate of intent to marry, which has to be witnessed by a J.P., lawyer, or medical doctor. This must then be authorized by the Australian Consulate in your nearest state capital or city. It's wise to contact the Australian Embassy or Consulate prior to making any arrangements for your wedding

documents required

- Birth certificate
- Passport
- ETA (Electronic Travel Visa) required. An ETA is an electronically stored authority to travel to Australia and can be obtained online at www.ETA.immi. gov.au or through participating travel agencies or airlines
- Divorce decree if divorced
- Death certificate of former spouse and previous marriage certificate if widowed
- Legal proof if name has been changed

Enjoy contemporary Australian cuisine and local produce with Asian influences.

The intense turquoise seas and lush mountain pastures create a stunning background for weddings. Marry barefoot on the private Old Settlement Beach or add a dash of charm to your ceremony and say "I do" under a protective roof of ancient trees.

When all is signed and sealed, champagne and canapés are served.

ABOVE

The clear waters at Old Settlement Beach.

———

LEFT

Enjoy the intimacy and tranquility of Arajilla.

———

TOP RIGHT

Recharge and unwind in the Banyan Suite.

Choose one of the stunning locations around the retreat for these tantalizing cocktails. Then there's a gourmet wedding breakfast awaiting, set amid the tropical surroundings of the restaurant.

There's plenty to do to while away the days on Lord Howe Island. Explore the lush rain forests, climb mountain peaks, or just take an Arajilla gourmet picnic basket to wherever your fancy takes you. There's also a wide range of water sports to enjoy. But if you prefer to take it easy, relax on a sunset cruise, get a fresh angle on the lagoon with a trip in a glassbottom boat, or just lounge around on one of the beautiful secluded beaches.

BRIDAL FILE

- *Weddings take place on beach, coves on the island, or private deck*
- *Ceremony conducted by celebrant*
- *Day spa*
- *Hair stylist, manicurist, masseur, makeup artist*
- *Photographer*

the observatory hotel
SYDNEY
NEW SOUTH WALES

"the best of everything"

Imagine a place with all the excitement of a city—great bars and restaurants, wonderful shops and elegant hotels—plus the luxury of scenery and beaches. It's hard to believe that such a place exists until you visit Sydney. This is a city with a vibrant urban culture and a hip beach life. Catch the sun's rays or go swimming, wander around historic cobbled quays, take a romantic sunset cruise around the harbor, or indulge in some designer-label shopping—Sydney has the best of everything.

Sydney is like no other city in the world. If you choose this "down under" destination, you won't be disappointed. You'll never be short of things to do; in fact, every day will bring a new adventure.

The sight of the magnificent Harbour Bridge, the amazing Sydney Opera House, and the spectacular Sydney skyline will take your breath away. Bondi Beach, famous not only for its surf but for its funky bars and cafés, is a great place to relax and watch the world go by.

Two hours away are the Megalong Valley and the Blue Mountains. The Three Sisters have to be seen to be believed, especially during the evening when the rock formations are magically lit against the night sky.

Like all major cities Sydney has a variety of locales, all with their own unique culture. The Rocks was the site of the first settlement and is now packed with nice old pubs, shops, and places to eat. Wander through cobbled streets and you'll discover historic buildings, each with its own tale to tell.

The hotel is near the Rocks and only a short distance from the city center.

BOTTOM LEFT

An elegantly appointed
Junior Suite.

—

LEFT

Enjoy afternoon tea in
the courtyard.

—

BELOW

The scenic Megalong Valley.

VITAL STATISTICS

rooms 100 rooms/suites

email email@observatoryhotel.com.au

website www.orient-express.com

legal requirements

- The couple must complete a certificate
  of intent to marry, which has to be
  witnessed by a J.P., lawyer, or medical
  doctor. This must then be authorized by
  the Australian Consulate in your nearest
  state capital or city. It's wise to contact
  the Australian Embassy or Consulate
  prior to making any arrangements for
  your wedding.

documents required

- Birth certificate
- Passport
- Divorce decree if divorced
- Death certificate of former spouse and
  previous marriage certificate if widowed
- Legal proof if name has been changed
- See page 72 for ETA information

The perfect place for a wedding and honeymoon, The Observatory Hotel is amazingly quiet, has wonderful views over Observatory Hill and Walsh Bay, and is convenient for exploring exciting Sydney.

The 100 rooms and suites are spacious and elegant. Some suites have balconies with beautiful views over the harbor and Sydney skyline.

BRIDAL FILE

- *Onsite wedding coordinators*
- *Wedding packages*
- *Ceremony conducted by celebrant*
- *Marriages take place in the Drawing Room*
- *Music: to suit couple's choice*
- *Spa, gym*
- *Hair stylist, manicurist, masseur, makeup artist*
- *Photographer & videographer*
- *Individually designed cake*
- *Flowers & boutonnieres*
- *Floral table decorations*
- *Separate room for the bride and groom to prepare for the wedding*

All individual in character, the rooms are luxuriously furnished with king-size beds, relaxing sitting areas, and marble bathrooms with oversize tubs.

ABOVE

Unwind in the pool or in the day spa and health and leisure club.

———

TOP RIGHT

The hotel's most spectacular suite is intimate, luxurious, and filled with objets d'art.

———

LEFT

Bathrooms are decadently spacious.

———

BOTTOM RIGHT

Breakfast on the terrace.

The hotel is renowned throughout Australia for its fine food. The Galileo Restaurant with its fine tapestries, crystal chandeliers, and walnut furniture combines quiet elegance with the informality of a typical Sydney restaurant. If you're seeking a relaxing haven within the hotel, the Globe Bar is the answer, and if you can't make it for lunch, then try their famous traditional afternoon tea served with a flute of champagne.

When it's time to chill out, swim in the indoor heated pool, mirrored by a ceiling of lights designed to re-create the constellations of the southern hemisphere, or pamper yourself in the day spa with its range of inviting treatments.

The Observatory Hotel is one of Sydney's most sought-after wedding venues. There are three wedding coordinators, and wedding packages are available.

Marriages take place in the Drawing Room, which has the feel of a 19th-century grand Australian home, and are conducted by a celebrant.

After the ceremony you can celebrate your marriage by taking a sunset cruise around the harbor or even an exhilarating helicopter trip before enjoying a candlelight dinner in the restaurant.

During your honeymoon there are lots of romantic adventures to be had. Take a secluded beach picnic by seaplane and soak up the privacy of your own private beach, fly to the Hunter Valley and enjoy a sumptuous dinner at a famous winery, or visit the Sydney Observatory and officially name a star that will forever celebrate your special day.

couran cove island resort
SOUTH STRADBROKE ISLAND
QUEENSLAND

"a classic daydream"

Lazy days of sun and surf combined with vibrant nights of excitement and action—this is what makes Australia's Gold Coast one of the most alluring wedding and honeymoon destinations. Waves from the broad blue Pacific Ocean break onto golden beaches under a subtropical sun. Venture inland from the beaches and a totally different picture unfolds—the green behind the gold: a world of tropical rain forests, rock pools, waterfalls, and glorious hidden treasures.

South Stradbroke Island is one of Australia's rare and unique sand islands. Undeveloped and with an unspoiled beauty, it boasts a vigorous diversity of flora and fauna, some of which are found nowhere else in the world.

Situated between Brisbane and the Gold Coast, South Stradbroke Island is just a short ferry trip away from the mainland and offers a combination of the best Australian beaches and bushland.

LEFT
Deluxe accommodation overlooking the resort's marina.

———

TOP RIGHT
Newlyweds amid the spectacular backdrop of the Cabbage Tree rain forest.

———

BOTTOM RIGHT
A marine suite lounge perched at the water's edge.

Its western beaches are calm and tranquil. Protected by the island from ocean waves, the stillness of the lagoon-like water provides the perfect backdrop for a truly spectacular Gold Coast sunset. In contrast the eastern beaches with their world-famous surf breaks, mountainous sand dunes, and spectacular expanse of the Pacific Ocean have a sensational outlook.

BRIDAL FILE

- *Onsite wedding coordinator*
- *2 wedding packages*
- *Weddings take place in Mango Chapel or on beach*
- *Ceremony conducted by celebrant*
- *Music: DJ, string bands, jazz bands, juke boxes*
- *Day spa, gym*
- *Hair stylist, beauty therapist, manicurist, masseur, makeup artist*
- *Photographer & videographer*
- *Individually designed cake*
- *Flowers & boutonnieres*
- *Floral table decorations*
- *Separate room for the bride and groom to prepare for the wedding*

Couran Cove Island Resort, set in peaceful surroundings, is a great destination for couples wanting something extraordinary on their wedding day or honeymoon.

From its 14 miles of unspoiled, patrolled beaches to the ancient rain forest, the natural environment is all-encompassing, with boardwalks that lead you over sand dunes, through lush vegetation, and right to the door of your own honeymoon haven.

The resort's 357 waterfront rooms and suites have an intimate, relaxed yet luxurious feel and are tastefully furnished to give an ambience that enhances the environment.

There are more than 100 different activities on offer at the resort, from water sports, kayak mangrove adventures, nocturnal and rain forest walks to parasailing and champagne cruises.

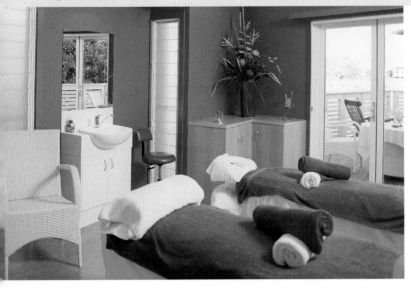

LEFT
Pampering at the day spa.

———

ABOVE
Take a ride in a buggy after
your wedding ceremony.

———

BELOW
The silk-draped interior
of the Pavilion party tent.

———

RIGHT
Tranquil perfection at the
Mango Chapel.

For a true taste of the island take a 4WD tour and discover the island's natural delights as your guide drives you through forested inland tracks to a secluded beach.

If you want to chill out, there's the day spa with a full range of treatments in the most relaxing environment you could ever find.

Poolside is a classic daydream. Laze the day away on a lounger while a waiter serves you cooling drinks and snacks.

Dining choices are numerous at Couran Cove. Choose from the resort's signature restaurant overlooking the marina, the Boardwalk Bar and Café, or the Spa Island Restaurant & Café with its 360-degree view of the lagoon.

Whether it's a wedding on a secluded beach with the sand between your toes or an intimate ceremony under a canopy of mango trees in the idyllic Mango Chapel, Couran Cove is a hideaway in which to celebrate your love together.

The hotel has a wedding coordinator to take care of all your arrangements and offers two wedding packages. Marriages are performed by a celebrant who will tailor the ceremony to your wishes.

Afterward, you can celebrate your wedding with a reception in the Surf Club before returning to your room, where champagne and chocolates await.

Couran Cove Island Resort is just on the doorstep of numerous world attractions. Travel through the Lamington National Park region en route to the famous O'Reilly's guest house and go tree-top walking, sample local wines, and take in the breathtaking scenery.

Take a trip to one of the major Gold Coast shopping centers, visit Conrad Jupiters Casino where you can wine, dine, and see the latest live show, or take a scenic helicopter or seaplane flight over some of the Gold Coast's most spectacular sites.

VITAL STATISTICS

rooms 357 rooms/suites

email
weddings@couran.com

website www.couran.com

legal requirements

- The couple must complete a certificate of intent to marry, which has to be witnessed by a J.P., lawyer, or medical doctor. This must then be authorized by the Australian Consulate in your nearest state capital or city. It's wise to contact the Australian Embassy or Consulate prior to making any arrangements for your wedding.

documents required

- Birth certificate
- Passport
- Divorce decree if divorced
- Death certificate of former spouse and previous marriage certificate if widowed
- Legal proof if name has been changed
- See page 72 for ETA information

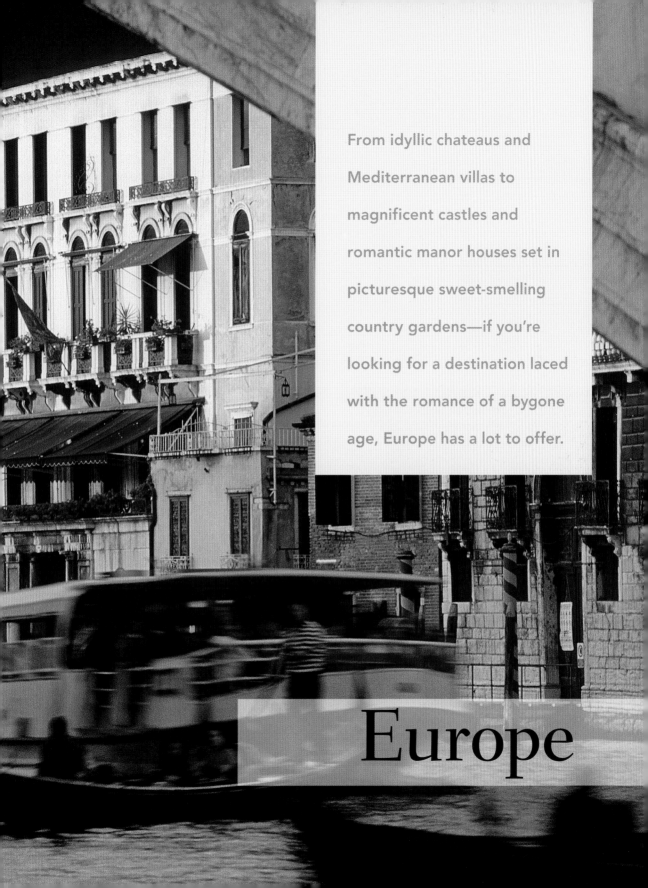

From idyllic chateaus and Mediterranean villas to magnificent castles and romantic manor houses set in picturesque sweet-smelling country gardens—if you're looking for a destination laced with the romance of a bygone age, Europe has a lot to offer.

Europe

le manoir aux quat' saisons
OXFORD
ENGLAND

"a pastoral scene made for lovers"

Rolling landscapes, dry-stone walls, historic churches, and sparkling clear streams—the Cotswolds represents an area that is forever England. Imagine tiny villages and hamlets seemingly unchanged with the passing of time. Thatched limestone houses set in fragrant flower gardens mingle with charming old-world tea shops and inns. Rustic bridges span meandering brooks and streams, while ancient oak trees stand majestically on pristine village greens, creating a pastoral scene made for lovers.

BRIDAL FILE

- *Wedding coordinator*
- *Weddings take place in the Milton Room or the superior suites*
- *Ceremony conducted by registrar*
- *Acoustic music*
- *Hair stylist, beauty therapist, manicurist, masseur, makeup artist*
- *Photographer & videographer*
- *Individually designed cake*
- *Flowers & boutonnieres*
- *Floral table decorations*
- *Separate room for the bride and groom to prepare for the wedding*

The Cotswolds is one of the most beautiful parts of the English countryside. Situated in middle England this peaceful, tranquil area is the perfect backdrop for weddings and honeymoons. The scenic beauty of the Cotswolds is as unique as its sleepy pace of life and restful ambience.

The Dovecote is situated between the main courtyard and the gardens.

——

BELOW

The Lavande Suite features a bay window overlooking the garden and has its own woodburning fire.

Every village is a piece of English history with its own tale to tell. And approximately 8 miles southeast of the city of Oxford, in a fold of low hills overlooking the rich water meadows of the Thames Valley, is the village of Great Milton.

The village has never been on a main road so has always been secluded; it remains comparatively unspoiled, growing old with grace while retaining some traces of each stage of its ancient history, which dates back to the 13th century.

The ancient church, timber-frame and thatched cottages, and many beautiful stone and stucco houses all bear witness to the attraction of the village as a dwelling place throughout the ages.

Great Milton is home to one of the finest hotels in England. Set amid magnificent gardens, Le Manoir aux Quat' Saisons is a 15th-century Cotswold house that has elegance, romance, and style.

VITAL STATISTICS

rooms 32 rooms/suites

email guestservices@blanc.co.uk

website www.manoir.com

legal requirements

- Couples must give notice of intention to marry no more than 1 year before or no less than 17 working days before they plan to marry at the registrar's office in the district in which they reside
- Couples must be resident in the district where they wish to marry for 7 days before the ceremony
- Couples must appear in front of the Oxford registrar in person
- Those resident outside the U.K. are advised to check the legalities for marriage with the authorities at home

documents required

- Passport
- Birth certificate
- Divorce decree if divorced
- Death certificate of former spouse if widowed
- For couples living outside the U.K. documentation (marriage visa or certificate of approval) will be required for the right to marry in the U.K.

The hotel's 32 rooms and suites are luxury personified. Each is individually designed and many have their own private terrace garden and views of the grounds. Design influences range from contemporary, Asian, and rustic to classical, and the rooms are adorned with sumptuous fabrics and furnishings. There is even a suite that features a stunning bathroom with a Botticelli mural and twin bathtubs.

Dining at the hotel is the experience of a lifetime. The modern French menu at the award-winning restaurant has been described as "a twist of imaginative genius" and the cuisine is the focus of every guest's visit.

The hotel has a wedding coordinator and ceremonies are performed by a registrar.

LEFT

Dine in the perfectly intimate setting of Le Manoir's restaurant.

——

BELOW

Situated in the garden courtyard, the Eugenie Suite has a contemporary edge on a rustic French provincial theme.

——

RIGHT

A lavender-scented stroll through the quintessentially English gardens.

ABOVE
Decadent bathing in the
Botticelli Suite.

Marriages take place in several different locations within the hotel. The Milton Room, with its oak panelling and sophisticated decor gives the feel of a great house of the past. Or you may choose to tie the knot in one of the four superior suites. The Lace Suite with its modern, feminine feel is based on traditional design and has a terrace with a water feature, while Lemongrass is a quietly sophisticated suite inspired by Southeast Asia. The Peony Suite has a contemporary yet classical style with a terrace leading to the main gardens, and Opium is an atmospheric haven with many Asian influences and its own walled garden with a stunning water feature.

After your wedding you can celebrate with champagne on your private terrace in the stillness of the evening and watch the sun go down before experiencing a gourmet candlelight dinner.

The hotel is surrounded by wonderful countryside and, as for places to visit, you will be spoiled for choice. Explore Oxford and take a trip on the river in a quintessential wooden punt, or just meander down the green country lanes through the picturesque villages.

Le Manoir can provide a hamper with a delicious picnic for you to put in the car before you leave. Then when you find the perfect spot, just stop the car, lay down the picnic blanket, and take in the breathtaking views.

hotel kämp

HELSINKI

FINLAND

"the perfect place to tie the knot"

Fairytale castles, a thousand lakes, and boundless culture—Finland is a country with a romantic appeal. From its spa towns and lakeland cities to its lively capital, this is the world as nature intended—unpolluted, invigorated, and safe.
Stay in an idyllic log cabin with an open fire and sauna nearby, tucked away from the rest of the world, or venture into Finnish Lapland and discover the Land of the Midnight Sun—Finland's romantic diversity makes it the ideal wedding destination.

Finland's capital, Helsinki, is a city of alluring contrasts where traditional eastern exotica meets contemporary western ways. Known as the Daughter of the Baltic, it is a neoclassical marvel and an intriguing mix of old and new.

The capital is essentially a peninsula; it's virtually surrounded by sea. Everywhere you turn there's water dotted with enchanting little islands. The sea brings with it rugged shorelines, soft beaches, near-untouched islands, seaside saunas, and glorious seafood.

Helsinki's cultural life is renowned for its quality and diversity. Eat in one of more than 700 restaurants, experience art, opera, haunting folk music, ballet, or jazz, or dance the night away in one of the excellent clubs.

This is the perfect place to tie the knot before embarking on a voyage of discovery where Finland's wonders will unfurl.

In the center of the capital overlooking the Esplanade Park, steeped in history and old-world charm, is Finland's only five-star hotel. To call Hotel Kämp a grand hotel is an understatement. Rated as one of the world's top 100 hotels, it has played host to royalty and the rich and famous since the 19th century.

The 179 guest rooms have been furnished to retain the original character of the hotel, but at the same time to have every modern facility and dreamlike refinement. Romantic decorations, king-size beds, spacious seating areas, large marble bathrooms—some with their own private sauna—make these rooms the very best in Scandinavia.

In the most fascinating and oldest part of the hotel are spacious specialty suites—the Mannerheim Suite is the biggest in Northern Europe.

On the eighth floor of the hotel is the Palace Kämp day spa. With its tranquil atmosphere it offers a comprehensive list of face and body treatments, massages, a gym, and a choice of saunas, including an intimate eucalyptus-fragrance grotto steam sauna.

There's an eclectic mix of dining facilities at the hotel. Choose from a lively restaurant with classical yet creative food or a modern Japanese restaurant. The Kämp Café & Bar terrace, open only in spring and summer, is the ideal place to eat alfresco.

BOTTOM LEFT

The palatial splendor of the Mannerheim Suite.

—

ABOVE

Enjoy European-style dining in the Kämp Café & Bar.

LEFT

The grand interior of the stunning Mirror Room.

BELOW

A sweeping balcony overlooks the hotel lobby.

BRIDAL FILE

- *Wedding package*
- *Weddings take place in the Mirror Room*
- *Ceremony conducted by government official in hotel, church ceremony by minister of religion*
- *Music: a variety of singers, artistes, and bands available*
- *Spa, gym, beauty salon*
- *Hair stylist, beauty therapist, manicurist, masseur, makeup artist*
- *Separate room for the bride and groom to prepare for the wedding*

Weddings at Hotel Kämp are lavish affairs and ceremonies take place in the Mirror Room. With its crystal chandeliers and gold decorations it resembles an 18th-century French salon with a huge mirror standing majestically at the far end of the room.

However, if you are looking for a unique wedding venue in Helsinki, Temppeliaukio Church is a stunning option and transportation can be arranged from the hotel. The Church of the Rock, as it's often called, is built into solid rock. It has an ambience like no place else, with natural light filtering into the building through 180 tiny glass windows between the wall and the dome.

VITAL STATISTICS

rooms 179 rooms/suites

email sales@hotelkamp.fi

website www.hotelkamp.fi

legal requirements & documents required

- Couples must provide official evidence that there aren't any legal or other reasons why they can't get married. This evidence should be issued by public authorities of their home country
- Passport
- Divorce decree if divorced
- Death certificate of former spouse if widowed
- For those wanting a church wedding, both parties need to provide proof of belonging to a Christian church in the form of an official document signed by a priest or church minister

ABOVE LEFT

The ceiling of the Church of the Rock is made of copper and is framed by 180 windows.

———

ABOVE

The exterior of the church was excavated from the rock.

Helsinki is easy and safe to explore on foot and makes an ideal starting point for a Finnish adventure. Visit Porvoo with its cobbled streets and tiny wooden houses. Explore the exquisite countryside or take the one-hour flight to Rovaniemi on the Arctic Circle—the reputed home of Santa Claus.

château de la chèvre d'or
ÈZE-VILLAGE
FRENCH RIVIERA

"the epitome of extravagance and style"

Backed by mountains and splashed by sunshine, the coastline of the Côte d'Azur is the most celebrated in the world. Warm seas lap onto sandy beaches, luxury yachts meander in and out of the tiny picturesque harbors of its famous towns, while echoes of an elegant past are mirrored in its magnificent architecture. This is the place that has lured the rich and famous for centuries with its glamor and grandeur—the ultimate destination for tying the knot.

The celebrated French Riviera is known worldwide for its glorious past, incredible wealth, and celebrity culture. The names of its towns are as famous as this piece of heaven that dips down into the Mediterranean.

St. Tropez is the epitome of extravagance and style and is one of the world's hot spots for pure glamour. Cannes spells out the ultimate in opulence, while Nice has a vibrant energy coupled with a grandeur of days gone by.

ABOVE

Soak up the sun by the pool overlooking the beautiful Côte d'Azur.

ABOVE
Each of the 33 rooms and
suites is unique.

———

TOP RIGHT
View from the chateau
to the Terrasse restaurant.

Along this stretch of coast lies the tiny principality of Monaco, one of the smallest states in Europe. Its history is as amazing as its year-round sparkling sunshine, and Monaco cleverly combines its colorful past with refined elegance, luxury hotels, sophisticated nightlife, and dazzling festivities.

Just 20 minutes from Nice and close to Monaco lies the Château de la Chèvre d'Or. The hotel is a jewel placed in the most beautiful setting of Eze, a medieval village and one of the most remarkable sites of the French Riviera.

Perched high up, overlooking the clear blue Mediterranean, the chateau is a wonderful location for weddings and honeymoons.

The hotel has 33 rooms and suites. Each room is unique and has its own original decor. One stretches over two floors, while another, bathed in sunlight, opens onto a patio at the side of the pool.

Some rooms are modern, others tell of a distant past—some are themselves a spectacle. The bathroom suite in one has a huge, round tub tucked under a rock from which there are spectacular views of mossy mountains and the greenery of the surrounding hills.

The dining experience at the chateau is sublime and an experience in the art of gastronomy. There are four restaurants to choose from. The large dining room has an exceptional panorama looking out over the Gulf of St. Tropez.

BRIDAL FILE

ABOVE

The Café du Jardin with its breathtaking view is perfect for lunch.

———

BELOW

The medieval entrance to the chateau.

———

RIGHT

The Exotic Garden overlooks the Gulf of St. Tropez.

The cherry woodwork on the walls casts a warm glow over the room, and the engraved glass motifs from the Belle Époque add a touch of fantasy to this picturesque setting. The Grill du Château is behind ramparts with wooden beams and has a magnificent view of the sea, while lunch on the scenic terrace under a white parasol, gazing out onto the blue water, is pure heaven.

For those who feel energetic there are a fitness club, heated swimming pool, sauna, and Jacuzzi, plus free entrance to the neighboring tennis club.

Marriages at the hotel take place in the gardens or in the early evenings in the Café du Jardin. Ceremonies are conducted by either a registrar or minister of religion. Although the hotel doesn't have a wedding coordinator, it's able to put couples in touch with wedding organizers in the Monte Carlo area. After the ceremony, in true French romantic style, couples can enjoy a candlelight dinner in their room or on their private terrace as they sit beneath the stars.

- *Weddings take place in the gardens or Café du Jardin*
- *Ceremony conducted by registrar or minister*
- *Music: to suit couple's choice*
- *Gym*
- *Hair stylist, beauty therapist, manicurist, masseur, makeup artist*
- *Photographer & videographer*
- *Individually designed cake*
- *Flowers & boutonnieres*
- *Floral table decorations*
- *Separate room for the bride and groom to prepare for the wedding*
- *Valet service*

If you can bear to tear yourself away from this perfect place, there are plenty of adventures awaiting, from a private boat trip along the coast to celebrity-spotting in nearby Nice or Monte Carlo.

VITAL STATISTICS

rooms 33 rooms/suites

email reservations@chevredor.com

website www.chevredor.com

legal requirements & documents required

There are complicated laws and requirements for couples wishing to marry in France. For full details of residency, legal documents, and procedures needed, contact the French Consulate in the state or city in which you reside. The complicated regulations mean that many couples choose to marry at home and combine a vow ceremony with their honeymoon

ashford castle
COUNTY MAYO
IRELAND

"luxury personified"

Discover a paradise that offers everything from a thrilling cultural voyage to nature's glorious wonderland. From ancient monuments to cosmopolitan cities, Ireland has so much to offer. Brace yourself for breathtaking scenery and seek out spectacular vistas, from soaring peaks and tranquil rivers fringed by green meadows to castles set beside pristine beaches, secluded coves, and picturesque fishing villages. The magical Emerald Isle with its slow pace of life has everything lovers need to make their special day complete.

Dramatically beautiful County Mayo is one of the least developed and most sparsely populated counties in Ireland. It's the place to escape the crowds and experience the unhurried pace of life on Ireland's west coast.

Mayo's landscape, with its undulating hills, untamed coast, and meandering rivers, provides an evocative backdrop for some of the most stunning locations in Ireland. From the windswept peaks to the crashing coast, it casts a spell like no other with clifftop views and white sandy beaches going hand in hand with poignant reminders of times past.

Mayo's tranquil towns are a joy to discover. Westport is a heritage town close to the rugged coast and full of character-laden pubs ringing with traditional music. Cong, with its traditional thatched cottages lining a babbling river bed, is known as the gateway to Connemara.

VITAL STATISTICS

rooms 83 rooms/suites
email sales@ashford.ie
website www.ashford.ie
legal requirements & documents required

- The laws for marrying in the Republic of Ireland are very complex so we suggest you contact the Irish Consulate in your nearest city for full details

LEFT
A fairytale setting for your wedding.

LEFT

Four-poster luxury in one of the state rooms.

———

BELOW

The opulent Connaught Dining Room.

ABOVE

Curl up in classic Georgian elegance.

Magnificent Ashford Castle, one of the finest and most luxurious hotels in Ireland, is located on the banks of the River Cong and set against a spectacular backdrop of forests, lakes, and mountains. Originally built as a castle in the 13th century and rebuilt as a hunting lodge in the 1800s, it became a hotel in 1939.

Since then Ashford Castle has welcomed and entertained its fair share of celebrities. Princess Grace and Prince Rainier, Ronald Reagan, John Wayne, Barbra Streisand, Jack Nicholson, and Brad Pitt to name but a few, have all enjoyed the hospitality of the castle.

The hotel's bedrooms are luxury personified and many retain their original features. Each is individually designed to provide stylish personal comforts, from the marble-tiled bathrooms to the sumptuous coordinated fabrics and furnishings.

And you can sleep like royalty in one of the carved oak four-poster beds in the luxurious state rooms.

Creative cooking, inspired ingredients, and an innovative menu are the key to Ashford's unique dining experiences. The 17th-century Connaught Dining Room, the most beautiful and intimate room in the castle, and the George V Room, with its gilded mirrors, chandeliers, candelabras, and sumptuous furnishings, are both perfect settings for a romantic dinner for two.

BRIDAL FILE

- *Onsite wedding coordinator*
- *Wedding blessing takes place in the walled gardens, by the lake, or in the Inglenook fireplace*
- *Ceremony conducted by a priest*
- *Transportation: horse-drawn carriage, vintage car, helicopter*
- *Music: to suit couple's choice*
- *Spa, gym, hair salon, beauty salon*
- *Hair stylist, beauty therapist, masseur*
- *Separate room for the bride and groom to prepare for the wedding*
- *Valet service*

External suppliers can be suggested for the following:
- *Photographer & videographer*
- *Flowers & boutonnieres*
- *Floral table decorations*

ABOVE

Indulge your senses in the health and beauty rooms.

——

BELOW

Falconry is one of the many activities available.

——

TOP RIGHT

Pre-reception drinks can be served in the baronial Oak Hall.

——

BELOW RIGHT

The perfect backdrop for a winter wedding.

In complete contrast, Cullen's at the Cottage, a short stroll across the river offers an informal option outside the castle while still on the estate.

And for guests who want to sample a traditional taste of Ireland, the Dungeon Bar has a harpist, singer, and nightly singalongs.

Although it's not possible to hold a civil or religious marriage ceremony in the castle, your fairytale wedding can begin with a blessing. However, wedding ceremonies can be conducted in the local churches. There's a Church of Ireland chapel on the estate and a Roman Catholic church on the edge of it, or you can drive 35 minutes to Ballintubber Abbey.

Blessings take place in the walled gardens, by the lake, or in the Inglenook fireplace and are conducted by a priest.

After the ceremony you can toast your life together with chilled champagne in your suite before dining in the sophisticated atmosphere of the George V Room.

The hotel offers a variety of sports and pursuits and has itineraries available for touring the nearby countryside, including a cocktail cruise on the lake to the Island of Inchagoill.

hotel cipriani
ITALY

"one of the most idyllic places on earth"

Follow in the footsteps of Casanova and be seduced by Venice, one of the most romantic cities in the world. Experience the magic of being serenaded with love songs in a gondola as you sail down winding waterways, passing under age-old bridges that have withstood the test of time. Meander down tiny cobbled streets, wonder at the architecture and beauty of balconied houses, palaces, and basilicas, or just sit and watch the world go by in some pristine piazza.

Venice is one of the most idyllic places on earth for a wedding and honeymoon.

It is a colorful, historic city that for centuries has beguiled and inspired poets, artists, authors, and some of the world's most significant fictional and real-life lovers.

The city is not overly large, and part of its charm lies in the fact that it takes just three or four hours to walk around the whole place, soaking up its sublime atmosphere.

Sites such as San Marco, with its magnificent piazza and basilica, and the Palazzo Ducale, where the Doges reigned supreme for century after century, evoke a sense of history like no other. But the jewels in Venice's crown are the canals that wind through the city and provide the ultimate romantic experience of being serenaded in a private gondola.

In the heart of the city, but gently removed from its hustle and bustle, is one of the world's most exclusive hotels. Hotel Cipriani is a luxurious and blissful retreat for weddings and honeymoons.

Its windows overlook the basin of San Marco, the Palladian church of San Giorgio, and the distant islands of the lagoon. Within the hotel's grounds are fabulous gardens that enchant and offer breathtaking views over the water.

Guests arrive at the hotel in a private launch, an overture to the elegance, style, and tranquility they will experience during their stay.

VITAL STATISTICS

rooms 46 rooms, 58 suites

email info@hotelcipriani.it

website
www.hotelcipriani.com

legal requirements & documents required

- The legalities are very complex for marrying in Venice. Marriages must take place in a registry office or church. A service of blessing, which is not legally valid, is the only one which can be performed in the hotel
- Most couples take the option of having a civil ceremony prior to a service of blessing in the location of their choice
- For full details of the marriage procedures, legalities, and documents required, contact the Italian Consulate in the state or city in which you reside

LEFT
Arrive in style in a private launch.

———

TOP
The elegant sitting room of the Palladio Suite.

The 46 rooms and 58 suites are truly luxurious. They range from simply elegant to those richly furnished with antiques and beautiful artworks. For an extra-special experience, the Dogaressa Suite, with its 18th-century antique furnishings and works of art, pink marble bathroom and four Gothic windows with stunning views, is hard to beat anywhere in the world.

The Hotel Cipriani dining experience is something to savor. The Fortuny Restaurant has mirrors, precious fabric decor, and views of the lagoon, and is the perfect setting for that special dinner, while the Fortuny Terrace is set in a lush, flowered garden. For alfresco dining the Gabbiano Poolside Restaurant beside the Olympic pool enables you to view Venice without even leaving your seat.

The Casanova Beauty and Wellness Center is named after the legendary 18th-century lover who once held clandestine trysts in the hotel's gardens. It provides a range of relaxing and pampering treatments, and incorporates a fitness room.

Although Italian law prevents couples from marrying in any other place than a church or registry office, you can hold a blessing ceremony at the hotel.

ABOVE

Grand interiors abound in the hotel's suites and rooms.

—

LEFT

The view over the water from the Dogaressa Suite.

—

TOP RIGHT

Luxurious living accommodation.

—

RIGHT

Say your vows in the tranquil beauty of the Casanova Gazebo.

Hotel Cipriani can supply a list of wedding coordinators who will arrange the civil or church ceremony and any other aspects of the wedding.

The Antique Garden, Casanova Gazebo, and Granaries of the Venetian Republic are the most beautiful places for blessing ceremonies at the hotel and have been the scene of marriage celebrations of the rich and famous.

And of course what could be more romantic than to celebrate your marriage with a romantic gondola ride followed by dinner in the privacy of your own suite? As the Venetians would say, "That's *amore*."

BRIDAL FILE

- *Blessing ceremonies take place in the Antique Garden, Casanova Gazebo, Granaries of the Venetian Republic*
- *Ceremony conducted by religious officiant*
- *Music: taped, local musicians playing traditional music, solo classical/modern singer, piano, string trio or quartet*
- *Spa, gym, hair salon*
- *Hair stylist, beauty therapist, manicurist, masseur, makeup artist*
- *Valet service*

External suppliers can be suggested for the following:
- *Photographer & videographer*
- *Individually designed cake*
- *Flowers & boutonnieres*
- *Floral table decorations*

ardanaiseig hotel
KILCHRENAN
SCOTLAND

"stately and timeless"

Savor the atmosphere of the Hebridean islands, the charm of rural villages, and the natural frontier that separates the rugged grandeur of the West Highlands from the gentler beauty of the Lowlands. Trace the footsteps of heroes like William Wallace, Robert the Bruce, and Mary, Queen of Scots. Glimpse an eagle, osprey, or fine antlered stag, or enjoy the spectacle of the Highland Games. Whatever you choose, the unspoiled landscape of glens and bays offers the ideal backdrop for a wedding or honeymoon.

VITAL STATISTICS

rooms 16 rooms/suites

email ardanaiseig@clara.net

website www.ardanaiseig.com

legal requirements

- There is no period of residency required to be married at Ardanaiseig, but the marriage does need to be registered 15 working days before the ceremony. The registrar also needs to be contacted at least 3 months in advance to arrange the required paperwork

documents required

- Birth certificate
- Passport
- Divorce decree if divorced
- Death certificate of former spouse if widowed
- Check with the registrar's office about the documents you need, including a marriage visa or certificate of approval

The West Highlands have a romantic ambience all their own. Over the centuries they have captivated artists, writers, and poets, including Sir Walter Scott whose poem "The Lady of the Lake" was inspired by the beauty of this area.

The countryside is some of the grandest in Scotland. At every turn the sea-fringed landscape is steeped in history. From the clear waters of Loch Awe, with its many islands and ancient lake dwellings, the landscape rises through forest, moor, and heather to the high summit of Ben Cruachan.

Set amid this spectacle of natural beauty lies Ardanaiseig, a Scottish baronial manor built in 1834. Since then not much has changed. Indeed, the stately and timeless atmosphere of the house, with its log fires, freshly cut flowers, and original antique furniture, persuades the visitor that the hustle and bustle of the 21st century is far away.

Ardanaiseig is a wonderful place for weddings and honeymoons. The exterior of this heritage property remains unchanged and the hotel retains the atmosphere of a private house. The 100-acre wild woodland gardens of Ardanaiseig are regarded as one of the natural splendors of Argyll and have their own romantic charm.

FAR LEFT
Carpets of bluebells lead to the hotel in spring.

———

TOP LEFT
The traditional decor of the Cruachan bedroom.

———

ABOVE
Warm yourself by the fire in the drawing room.

———

BELOW
The stunning view across Loch Awe.

BRIDAL FILE

- *Onsite wedding coordinator*
- *Ceremony conducted by registrar or minister*
- *Marriages take place in the drawing room or lochside amphitheater*
- *Transportation: horse-drawn carriage, vintage car*
- *Music: local musicians, piper, solo modern/classical singer, taped music, organ/piano, string trio or quartet*
- *Photographer & videographer*
- *Individually designed cake*
- *Flowers & boutonnieres*
- *Floral table decorations*
- *Separate room available for bride and groom to prepare for the wedding.*
- *Valet service*

External suppliers can be suggested for the following:
- *Beauty therapist, manicurist, masseur, makeup artist*

Spend an unforgettable night in one of the 16 bedrooms, which are furnished with antiques and works of art, and named after local mountains, glens, lochs, and castles. The ideal honeymoon haven is the converted boatshed with its breathtaking views over the loch to Ben Lui, one of the finest locations on the west coast of Scotland. The double-height windows allow you to enjoy the outside without the need to move from your own sitting room, while the mezzanine bedroom, with its glass balustrade, offers an uninterrupted view over the loch.

Dine in the restaurant, which overlooks the lawns running down to the loch and is one of the best in the Highlands. It is decorated with fine paintings, the linen is crisp, the silver glints, and the crystal sparkles in the candlelight.

BELOW

A wedding with friends and family in the loch-side amphitheater.

——

RIGHT

The "get away from it all" converted boatshed—a wilderness honeymoon retreat.

Savor a full Scottish breakfast, and for afternoon tea on the croquet lawn, home-made breads, scones, and jam come into their own.

Marriages at Ardanaiseig can take place in the drawing room or out in the open-air lochside amphitheater. For a taste of true Scotland, a traditional piper can be provided at the ceremony. There is a wedding coordinator to help you plan your day and the ceremony can be conducted either by the registrar or local minister.

During your stay there are romantic adventures to be had, such as a boat trip to Loch Awe with a picnic basket for two, stopping off on Inishail Island. Or indulge yourself in a private sight-seeing tour with the hotel's own chauffeur and car.

Loch Ness, Loch Lomond, and the Victorian port of Oban with regular ferries to the beautiful islands of Skye, Mull, and Iona are all within easy reach.

icehotel
JUKKASJÄRVI
SWEDEN

"the ultimate ice palace"

Every winter a new hotel created from ice and snow rises up in Jukkasjärvi. Created from the frozen, wild, and crystal clear waters of the Torne River, the Icehotel is the largest hotel of its type in the world. With its ethereal ambience and palatial splendor created by the mix of modern design and traditional architectural expertise, it's easy to understand why it's often described as a "hotel built of dreams." So live your dream in this winter wonderland.

Imagine the setting for a wedding so romantically unique that it could have come from the pages of a fairytale.

A hotel made of ice and snow conjures up stark, spartan images of a bleak, soulless property, but in the case of the Icehotel nothing could be further from the truth—this property is a work of art.

BELOW
After a night cozily wrapped up on a bed of reindeer skins, you are wakened with a glass of warm lingonberry juice.

Arches inspired by historic cathedrals form the main core of the majestic structure. Ice pillars, chandeliers, designer ice furniture, ice sculptures, and even a winter garden created by a leading landscape architect make this the ultimate ice palace.

There's a certain magic about this place—a magic that sees couples coming from all over the world to hold their weddings in the Ice Chapel on the Torne River. So if you're thinking of making your vows in this unique and surreal environment, it's best to contact the hotel ahead of time.

The hotel has a wedding coordinator who will assist in providing the legal requirements, such as an investigation into possible impediments. This involves a formal visit to the tax office in Kiruna to obtain the necessary certificate.

ABOVE

A Russian art nouveau
ice feature.

———

LEFT

The hotel changes design
and layout each year, with
artists creating unique ice
sculptures in all the rooms.

BRIDAL FILE

- *Onsite wedding coordinator*
- *Ceremony conducted by priest*
- *Marriages take place in the Ice Chapel*
- *Transporation: vintage cars, limousines*
- *Music: local musicians playing traditional music*
- *Photographer*
- *Individually designed cake*
- *Flowers & boutonnieres*
- *Floral table decorations*

And so to bed. The Icehotel has several types of accommodation. The ideal is to combine a cold night in the Icehotel with several warm nights in the Kaamos rooms in order to fully enjoy the experience. But for that night to remember, a deluxe suite is the epitome of sharing a surreal night with someone special.

The suites are decorated with ice and art sculptures, and the door can be locked. You sleep in a thermal sleeping bag on a special bed of ice and snow, on reindeer skins. In the morning you're awakened with a cup of lingonberry juice at your bedside and can enjoy a morning sauna and buffet breakfast.

The warm accommodation is cozy and inviting in light, newly built double rooms with corner windows to take in the magnificent views.

LEFT
Absorb the heat of a roaring log fire while dining.

——

BELOW
The inviting warmth of a Kaamos room.

VITAL STATISTICS

rooms Cold accommodation:
   deluxe and ordinary suites,
   double rooms (around 80)
   Warm accommodation:
   44 double bedrooms and
   28 family rooms with private
   bathrooms

email info@icehotel.com

website www.icehotel.com

**legal requirements &
documents required**

- Couples need to visit
   the local tax office in
   Kiruna for a certificate
   regarding consideration of
   impediments. Contact your
   wedding coordinator
   for details

For a romantic dinner choose between the award-winning Icehotel Restaurant—not made of ice—where gourmet meals are served on plates made of crystal-clear ice, or the historic Old Homestead Restaurant dating from the 18th century, 800 yards away overlooking the Torne River.

The Icehotel abounds with adventures and activities to make your stay truly memorable. However, do book your activities and excursions at least three weeks before your arrival as they fill up quickly.

In the surroundings of the Icehotel you can experience ice sculpting and see the results of your own creativity, take a snowshoe or cross-country ski excursion, or try Saab Ice Driving to improve your driving skills. There are also snowmobile and husky safaris if you want a longer outdoor experience.

In the evening there are performances of stories and traditional folk singing under the stars and the northern lights in a traditional-style tent on the shores of the Torne River. You shouldn't miss this experience.

ABOVE
Chill out in the ice bar.

Live the dream with a
marriage made in paradise.
There could be nothing more
romantic than the idea of
exchanging your vows on
a beautiful tropical island
against a background of azure
blue seas, swaying palm trees,
and exotic flowers.

Islands

one&only ocean club
PARADISE ISLAND
BAHAMAS

"luxury love nest"

Island life is a dream existence that many would like to try. Tie the knot and spend your honeymoon in the Bahamas and the dream can become a reality. It's easy to fall in love with these islands. Wander lazily along miles of pink sandy beaches. Swim, snorkel, or dive in their beautiful crystal-clear seas. Dine under the stars with the ocean lapping at your feet. Whatever you choose, it will be love at first sight.

Christopher Columbus famously avoided the ocean around the Bahamas because of its shallow, clear water, but today thousands of tourists head here just for a sight of the absurdly blue water that surrounds these beautiful islands.

The 700 stunning islands and bays of the Bahamas stretch from just north of the Greater Antilles, across the Tropic of Cancer, and up alongside the coast of Florida.

Truly a tropical paradise, no day is ever the same on these enchanting islands. Opt for the glitz and glamour of Nassau on New Providence Island, Grand Bahama or Paradise Island or escape to the Out Islands, where life moves at a slower pace and it's easy to find a deserted beach to call your own.

Located on Paradise Island is the Bahamas's most prestigious hotel,

One&Only Ocean Club. It is set within the serenity of a private estate, and has all the discreet sophistication and colorful grandeur of days gone by. Legendary in its reputation for entertaining the world's elite for more than 45 years, it has an air of peace and tranquility that makes this a favorite celebrity retreat. Cindy Crawford held her wedding here.

You can follow suit and hold your celebration in the stunning gardens

ABOVE

Enjoy a meal at the Clubhouse, overlooking the breaking waves.

—

LEFT

Swaying palms on the Hartford Lawn.

—

FAR LEFT

A beautiful ocean view from your room.

BRIDAL FILE

- *Onsite wedding coordinator*
- *Wedding package*
- *Weddings take place on pool terrace, by the Augustinian Cloister, or in Versailles Gardens*
- *Ceremony conducted by marriage officer/minister*
- *Transportation: vintage or open-top car*
- *Music: local musicians playing traditional native music, solo classical/modern singer, taped music, organ/piano, string trio/quartet, calypso band, folk singers/musicians*
- *Spa, gym, hair salon, beauty salon*
- *Hair stylist, beauty therapist, manicurist, masseur, makeup artist*
- *Photographer & videographer*
- *Individually designed cake*
- *Flowers*
- *Floral table decorations*

inspired by the grandeur of Versailles. Exchange your vows among fragrant blossoms that grow beside steps graced by marble and bronze statues leading up to the dramatic arches of the 12th-century Augustinian Cloister, shipped over from Lourdes in the 1920s. The view of the bay is magnificent, especially at sunset.

The hotel's elegant 106 rooms and suites, all with views of the pristine blue ocean, have a warm, inviting ambience laced with contemporary luxury. Newlyweds are treated with special care. There's a romantic evening turndown service with a uniquely Bahamian twist, a Bath Ceremony and chilled bottles of champagne plus an intimate dining experience for two—on a beach with toes in the sand, at the beach deck under a starry sky, or amid the intoxicating beauty of the Versailles Gardens.

One&Only Ocean Club is renowned for its cuisine, and the Courtyard Terrace

VITAL STATISTICS

rooms 106 rooms/suites

email celebrations@ oneandonlyoceanclub.com

website www.oneandonlyresorts.com

legal requirements
- Residency 48 hours
- Local Bahamian bridal consultant is required to make wedding arrangements, including acquiring wedding license, registration and ceremony officials

documents required
- Passport
- Divorce decree if divorced
- Death certificate of former spouse if widowed
- Adoption certificate or legal proof of name if applicable

is one of the most romantic garden-setting restaurants in the Caribbean, where you can dine beneath the stars.

For ultimate indulgence visit the spa with its eight Balinese-style private treatment villas and its daybeds and jetted tubs in a private garden.

If you can tear yourself away from this luxury love nest, then spirited adventures and island excursions await. Swim with dolphins, tour historic Nassau in a horse-drawn carriage, or cruise to the Out Islands.

For an extravagant escape, consider a seaplane trip to an uninhabited island with absolute privacy, a gourmet picnic, a bottle of chillled champagne, and a beach without another living soul.

FAR LEFT

Dip your toes in the gently lapping waves on a deserted beach.

——

BELOW

Sip cocktails in the Dune Bar and watch the sun set.

southern cross club
LITTLE CAYMAN

"a match made in heaven"

CAYMAN ISLANDS

In the Cayman Islands, your very own slice of paradise is there for the taking. Set like sparkling jewels glistening in an emerald sea, this trio of islands has an idyllic tropical beauty. Dazzling white beaches, crystal-clear water, and the elegance and sophistication of a world-class destination are a match made in heaven. Whatever your passion, the Cayman Islands have the beauty and ambience for a quintessential island escape.

These three islands, each quite different in character, lie some 480 miles south of Miami and 180 miles to the northwest of Jamaica. Grand Cayman is the largest, measuring just 8 miles across at its widest. Rugged Cayman Brac is the second largest, and sleepy Little Cayman with a population of just over 100 is as close to a Robinson Crusoe-style getaway as you are likely to find.

One of the least developed, safest, and easily accessible tropical islands in the western hemisphere, Little Cayman entices visitors with its seclusion, the undeveloped beauty and extraordinary diversity of its marine environment, and the unspoiled tranquility of its land and beaches.

Over the years, many Caribbean islands have lost their natural scenery to overdevelopment, but on Little Cayman time has stood still.

The Cayman Islands are the essence of carefree Caribbean style and are the perfect retreat for any couple, especially those seeking a romantic spot for a tropical wedding or honeymoon.

VITAL STATISTICS

rooms 12 bungalows

email scc@candw.ky

website www.southerncrossclub.com

legal requirements

- Couples can marry on the same day
  as they arrive in the Cayman Islands
- They must have:
  a non-resident marriage license;
  a letter from the authorized marriage
  officer who is to officiate
- Applications for non-resident marriage
  licenses can be obtained from Deputy
  Chief Secretary's Office, Government
  Administration Building, 3rd Floor,
  George Town, Grand Cayman B.W.I.

documents required

- Proof of citizenship and age
- Divorce decree if divorced
- Death certificate of former spouse
  if widowed
- Cayman Islands Immigration
  Department pink entry slip

The casually sophisticated Southern Cross Club, with its 12 oceanfront bungalows, is spread across a 900-foot stretch of beautiful white-sand beach facing the South Hole Sound and Owen Island.

Each of these bungalows is individually designed. They have ocean views, outside decks, air-conditioning, and every amenity for your comfort. The honeymoon suite is on the eastern edge of the beachfront.

FAR LEFT

Tropical colors dominate in the cool interiors of the bungalows.

———

ABOVE

The pool deck next to the club's main building.

The stunning suite for honeymoon couples is the perfect setting for romance, with a private veranda that overlooks the uninhabited Owen Island. Watch the sun set over the turquoise Caribbean sea from your king-size bed or, for the ultimate romantic experience, from your private outdoor shower.

The Club's main building is set in the middle of the row of bungalows. Here, guests can enjoy an eclectic mix of Caribbean cuisine in the air-conditioned dining room, screened outdoor dining pavilion, on the pool deck, or on the beach under a bright Caribbean moon.

Scattered around the property, palm-thatched gazebos provide shade for dozens of hammocks—just the place to relax as the trade wind breezes cool the air and the sound of the waves gently breaking on the fringing reef drifts across South Hole Sound. Or you can step into the cooling and inviting interior of the special bamboo massage spa to experience the wonders of its treatment.

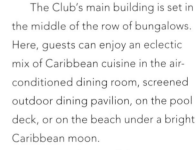

Weddings at the Southern Cross Club are sheer bliss. There's a wedding coordinator to help with your plans, and ceremonies are conducted by a Justice of the Peace or the local minister. You can pick your wedding site on arrival. Choose from the beach, under a palm tree, Little Cayman Church, on the pool deck, or be taken by pontoon boat to deserted Owen Island. After your nuptials, dine by candlelight on your private veranda or under a thatched hut on the beach.

During your stay you can indulge in a range of activities. Explore the lagoon or the nearby mangroves in a kayak, swim, snorkel, bicycle, or catch an outdoor movie under a billion tropical stars.

TOP LEFT

The Southern Cross Club's jetty at dusk.

———

BOTTOM LEFT

Room with a view.

———

BELOW

Shaded hammocks for lazy days.

BRIDAL FILE

- *Onsite wedding coordinator*
- *Wedding package*
- *Weddings take place on the beach, on deserted Owen Island, at Little Cayman Church, under a palm tree, or on the pool deck*
- *Ceremony conducted by local Justice of the Peace or local minister*
- *Music: local musicians playing traditional music, taped music, organist/pianist (in church only), local DJ*
- *Spa*
- *Hair stylist (available from Grand Cayman), beauty therapist, manicurist, masseur, makeup artist (available from Grand Cayman)*
- *Photographer & videographer*
- *Individually designed cake*
- *Flowers & boutonnieres*
- *Floral table decorations*
- *Valet service (available from Grand Cayman)*

longueville manor
JERSEY
CHANNEL ISLANDS

"an oasis of peace and tranquility"

They say that the best things come in small packages, and the island of Jersey is no exception. It has beautiful beaches, quiet country lanes, excellent hotels and restaurants, and more sun than anywhere else in the British Isles. It's within easy reach of the U.K. and mainland Europe, yet has a hideaway atmosphere that's perfect for a wedding and honeymoon destination.

Set in the sparkling waters of the Bay of St. Malo, Jersey is only 14 miles from the French coast and 100 miles from the south coast of England.

The largest and most southerly of the Channel Islands has naturally beautiful and varied scenery. Along the rugged northern coastline there are little harbors, coves, and secluded bays protected by towering granite cliffs.

The beaches on the south of the island have won some of the highest accolades. St. Brelades Bay, where colorful gardens stretch down to the ocean, has been described as one of the loveliest in the world. In contrast, you'll find magnificent sands on the west coast where Atlantic breakers crash onto the shores.

Exploring the interior of the island will lead you along quiet country lanes dotted with granite cottages and farms, and through meadows and woodlands.

FAR LEFT

Stay in luxurious style in
the Longueville Suite.

—

LEFT

The impressive entrance to
the 14th-century manor.

—

BELOW

Lighted by candles, the Oak
Room is a sophisticated
venue for your ceremony.

A network of green lanes, where
pedestrians get precedence over
the car, ensures that the country life
keeps an unhurried pace.

A short drive from St. Helier, the
capital, is Longueville Manor, a 14th-
century Norman manor house, which has
been lovingly restored and converted into
one of Europe's most celebrated hotels.

This oasis of peace and tranquility
is set in 15 acres at the foot of its
own beautiful, private wooded valley
complete with an enchanting lake, which
is home to majestic black swans.

It's just the place to sit back and
relax in amid a background of floral
displays, fine antiques, and furnishings,
and be pampered by attentive staff.

For the more active there are tennis
courts, croquet lawns, and a large
heated pool. There's also plenty of
space for a romantic stroll in the park
under the moon.

Longueville Manor's 31 bedrooms,
each named after a rose, are sanctuaries
where you can slip between Egyptian
cotton sheets, or recline in a chaise
longue with a magazine.

BRIDAL FILE

- *Onsite wedding coordinator*
- *3 wedding packages*
- *Weddings are held in the Oak Room*
- *Ceremony conducted by registrar*
- *Transportation: horse-drawn carriage, vintage car, open-top car*
- *Music: solo classical/modern singer, taped music, organ/piano, string trio or quartet, harpist*
- *Hair stylist, beauty therapist, manicurist, masseur, makeup artist*
- *Photographer & videographer*
- *Individually designed cake*
- *Flowers & boutonnieres*
- *Floral table decorations*
- *Separate room for the bride and groom to prepare for the wedding*
- *Valet service*

Anything you could possibly need for your comfort is only a wish away. The ground-floor rooms have private patios that look directly onto the gardens— just the place to sit with a glass of champagne and toast your life together.

Eating at Longueville Manor is without doubt an experience to be savored.

ABOVE

The cosy drawing room.

—

RIGHT

Champagne for two.

—

BOTTOM RIGHT

Share afternoon tea by the pool and gardens.

Sample the menu at the poolside bar or take a specially prepared picnic hamper to a secluded spot. In the evening, dine by candlelight in the oak-panelled dining room on award-winning cuisine served with fresh herbs and vegetables from the hotel's gardens.

Weddings at Longueville are perfection personified, tailored to each couple's requirements. Ceremonies take place in the elegantly sophisticated Oak Room and are conducted by a registrar.

The extensive gardens, with swans gliding serenely across the lake, provide a wonderful backdrop to celebrating your marriage in style with champagne and canapés, followed by a candlelight dinner in the restaurant.

Afterwards you can retire to the Longueville Suite, which is a romantic dream come true. Tucked away in your own turret, you will find an impressive four-poster bed, dressing room, and a hand-painted tub big enough for two.

During your honeymoon do take time out to explore the countless historic and diverse places on the island, and make sure you indulge in some tax-free shopping before you leave.

VITAL STATISTICS

rooms 31 rooms/suites

email

info@longuevillemanor.com

website

www.longuevillemanor.com

legal requirements

- Wedding applications can be made by mail to the office of the Superintendent Registrar, 10 Royal Square, St. Helier, JE2 4WA. Once the paperwork is complete, you need only arrive 3 working days before the wedding to complete the formalities
- Without a mail application you need to arrive 10 working days before the wedding

documents required

- Full copy of birth certificate
- Court sealed and certified copy of divorce decree if divorced
- A widow must produce her marriage certificate as well as death certificate of her late husband. A widower need only produce the death certificate of his late wife.
- Documents not in English must be accompanied by a certified English translation
- Contact the Immigration Department to check you have the necessary immigration clearance before coming to the island to be married

crown beach resort
RAROTONGA
COOK ISLANDS

"a unique romantic hideaway"

In the Cook Islands sugar-white beaches, sheltered lagoons, and green mountains reach down to the South Pacific's sparkling turquoise waters. Marry at sunset on a secluded beach surrounded by flaming torches, be carried aloft in a chair by native warriors, or arrive by canoe to a traditional drumbeat—this is the ultimate wedding destination for pure romantics.

Tiny and remote, the Cook Islands consist of 15 islands scattered over 850,000 square miles across the heart of the South Pacific like a string of natural pearls. Lying between Samoa, Fiji, and Tahiti, these islands are renowned for their stunning natural beauty.

Rarotonga is the main island of the southern Cooks and unquestionably one of the most attractive. It is an idyllic haven where you can relax on beautiful, clean white sandy beaches, and refresh yourself in shallow lagoons sealed off by a protective outer reef.

ABOVE

A secluded wedding in lush vegetation.

—

RIGHT

The muslin-draped wedding gazebo can also be the setting for a romantic dinner.

The Crown Beach Resort is spread over 4.5 lush acres, with cascading water features, a pristine white-sand beach, and breathtaking sunsets.

It offers 21 traditional thatched Polynesian-style luxury villas set within its tropical gardens.

BRIDAL FILE

- *2 onsite wedding coordinators*
- *3 wedding packages*
- *Weddings take place in the gardens or on the beach*
- *Ceremony conducted by Justice of the Peace or minister*
- *Transportation: a royal chair carried by warriors, traditional canoe*
- *Music: local village string band, serenader, choir, local village drummers, taped music*
- *Spa, gym, beauty salon*
- *Beauty therapist, manicurist, masseur*
- *Hair stylist, makeup artist by arrangement*

Avarua, the capital of the islands, is situated on Rarotonga. You can wander around the good range of shops, take time out to enjoy refreshment at some of the good bars and cafés, and watch the world go by in this charming place with a slow pace of life. On the northwestern sunset side of Rarotonga, just 10 minutes away from the capital, is a unique romantic hideaway.

Each villa is very private and has a kitchen for times when your plans include a romantic dinner just for two. There are king-size beds, and whisper-quiet air-conditioning keeps you cool.

Crown Beach offers dining styles and meal choices to tantalize all tastes. Whether it's the unparalleled ocean views of the Oceans Restaurant or the superior service at the widely acclaimed Windjammer Restaurant, your dining experience will be truly memorable.

TOP
Cool down by the cascading falls.

—

ABOVE
The Polynesian-style villas contain contemporary interiors.

ABOVE

Entertainment—Polynesian
style.

——

RIGHT

An island paradise made
for two.

——

TOP RIGHT

Enjoy the spectacular sunset
before dinner.

——

FAR RIGHT

The warm waters of the
South Pacific are only a few
steps away.

And for those wanting to dine in a more
intimate setting there's the memorable
experience of sharing dinner on the
beach with your own personal waiter
and serenader.

The My Beauty & Spa is a sanctuary
of beauty treatments and soothing
massages.

Weddings at this resort are like
no other. There are two onsite wedding
coordinators and three different
wedding packages.

Ceremonies take place on the
white-sand beach lit by flaming torches
with a sunset backdrop, in the gazebo
overlooking the lagoon, near the
freshwater swimming pool, or under
the resort's famous 150-year-old
Flamboyant tree.

Transportation to your wedding
is exotic. You both can be carried in a

VITAL STATISTICS

rooms 21 villas

email info@crownbeach.com

website www.crownbeach.com

legal requirements

- If under 21, written legal consent is
  required from parents/guardians.
- An application for a wedding license has
  to be made in person at least 3 working
  days before the wedding from the
  Registrar's Department in Avarua

documents required

- Passport
- Birth certificate
- Divorce decree if divorced
- Death certificate of former spouse
  if widowed

paata—a royal chair—by four warriors in traditional costume, or the bride can arrive at the wedding gazebo in a canoe.

Local village drummers can beat the traditional drums to welcome the bride, warriors can escort the bridal couple, or you can even hire a full Polynesian show, including string band, singers, dancers, and drummers.

Afterward, return to your villa where champagne, canapés, and a flower-covered bed await you. In the evening a champagne dinner will be served on your private balcony.

During your stay there's plenty to do. Go horseback riding, take a lagoon cruise, adventure out on a 4WD tour, or indulge in a couple's massage.

hotel katikies
SANTORINI
CYCLADES ISLANDS

"it's love at first sight"

Its extraordinary beauty has made Santorini the pearl of the Greek archipelago. For thousands of years famous poets have praised the volcanic island, adoring its natural beauty and exquisite scenery, where endless sea and infinite sky melt into one, lost together in the deepest blue, so brilliant it dazzles. Santorini has a mystical and romantic charm, and undoubtedly the most amazing sunsets in the whole of the Aegean, making it a dream wedding and honeymoon destination.

There are many ancient tales about Santorini. According to legend, this wonderful island was created by giant volcanic eruptions, which destroyed the lost island of Atlantis around 3,600 years ago. The volcano eventually sank back into the sea to create the world's largest volcanic bay—the steep cliffs on three sides of the bay are what remains of the crater walls.

The Aegean Sea, lapping the shores of Santorini's black-and red-sand beaches which rise into spectacular, wild rugged cliffs towering more than 1,000 feet high, has a transparency of light and a depth of color that creates unique emerald visions and awesome sunsets.

Picturesque villages nestle above the rock face with iconic snow-white houses, blue-domed churches, and thousands of zigzag steps, which are synonymous with the island.

Katikies, on the most westerly point of Santorini, is a legend among hotels in the Cyclades. Situated in the picturesque village of Oia, it's built against the cliffs, 300 feet above the dazzling blue caldera basin. This blissful haven is like no other, for it creates the magical feeling of being suspended between air and sea.

RIGHT

Perched on a cliff, the hotel commands exceptional views of the Aegean Sea.

—

BELOW

The simple interiors are cool and welcoming.

Savor your initial breathtaking glimpse of Katikies. Aegean architecture blends past with present in a free-form fantasy of stairs, bridges, cubist cottages, and infinity pools. Each of the 25 rooms and suites has its own sea-view balcony and is furnished with island antiques.

The honeymoon suite has everything you could expect of an Aegean love nest: a spacious bedroom, living room, and large panoramic terrace with lounge. There's an open-air dining area for those romantic candlelight dinners, a sundeck, and an outdoor Jacuzzi just made for two.

During the day you can swim in either of the two pools, lounge on the sunbathing deck with its open-air Jacuzzi,

BRIDAL FILE

- *Onsite wedding coordinator*
- *Wedding packages*
- *Weddings take place on the terrace*
- *Ceremony conducted by a marriage officer*
- *Transportation: vintage cars, limousines*
- *Music: taped music, DJ*
- *Spa available at sister hotel, Kirini, 600 yards away*
- *Hair stylist, beauty therapist, manicurist, masseur, makeup artist*
- *Photographer & videographer*
- *Individually designed cake*
- *Flowers & boutonnieres*
- *Floral table decorations*
- *Separate room for the bride and groom to prepare for the wedding*
- *Valet service*

ABOVE

A relaxing massage on the sunbathing deck next to the open-air Jacuzzi.

—

RIGHT

A romantic dinner in the Katikies Gourmet Dinner Restaurant with spectacular views of the caldera basin.

or just enjoy your favorite cocktail in the Pool Bar and relax to the sound of soft music and spectacular views.

Candlelight dinners are served in the open-air Katikies Gourmet Dinner Restaurant, or you may prefer a variety of Greek delicacies in the Pool Restaurant Kirini, with views of the volcano. At sunset you can participate in a ceremonial wine tasting of the famous Santorinian wines.

Although there are several wedding packages, the onsite wedding coordinator can also help to tailor things to your needs.

Ceremonies, conducted by a marriage officer, take place on the terrace overlooking the blue sea. After the ceremony you can take a ride in a horse-drawn carriage or a convertible for some quality alone time. Your celebration dinner will be served by candlelight on your own balcony. And you'll find champagne and canapés in your room, and the romantic touch of a bed covered in flowers.

Katikies provides some wonderful excursions. There are exclusive chauffeur-driven tours to the villages, beaches, and wineries, catamaran cruises to secluded islands, and the chance to sail at sunset with dinner served on board.

VITAL STATISTICS

rooms 25 rooms/suites

email info@katikies.com

website www.katikies.com

legal requirements

- For weddings in Greece most documents relating to your status must be translated into Greek. Translations can be done at your local Greek Consulate

documents required

- Passport
- Divorce decree if divorced
- Documents that require translation: Birth certificate and Single Status letter also known as Certificate of No Impediment. This can be obtained from your local government office/ Town Hall or County Clerk's Office. Both these documents must be authenticated by an apostille (a special letter and stamp). The apostille must be issued by the state/country where your document was issued, regardless of where you now reside

the intercontinental aphrodite hills resort hotel
KOUKLIA
CYPRUS

"romance is in the air"

Legend has it that Aphrodite, the goddess of love and beauty, rose from the foaming waves off the rocky southwest coast of Cyprus. Could there be a more romantic spot for lovers to marry than Paphos, the island capital in Roman times? Statues and mosaics remind you of the divine patron of marriage, and on a balmy, jasmine-scented evening, when the fiery sun drops like a huge tangerine coin into the blue Mediterranean, you can almost feel her presence.

BELOW

Relax in the poolside Jacuzzi.

———

TOP RIGHT

Enjoy the panoramic vista from the Village Square.

———

BOTTOM RIGHT

Indulge yourself with a spa treatment at The Retreat.

Cyprus is an island with spectacular scenery and a wonderful climate. Here cool, pine-clad mountains, golden beaches, lush vineyards and tranquil villages, go hand in hand with cosmopolitan towns. Greek temples, ancient Roman mosaics, and Byzantine monasteries tell the varied history of this magical island and are just waiting to be explored.

The third largest island in the Mediterranean stands at the crossroads of Africa, Asia, and Europe. Throughout the ages its strategic geographical location has made it very attractive to invaders. Each conquering culture has left its imprint on the island.

This unspoiled corner of Cyprus has always been synonymous with lovers. Richard the Lionheart married the beautiful Berengaria of Navarre in the

VITAL STATISTICS

rooms 290 rooms/suites

website www.aphroditehills.com,
www.intercontinental.com/aphrodite

legal requirements

- Minimum residence in Cyprus five days
  before the ceremony
- Couples need to visit the Town Hall
  prior to the wedding to complete the
  application for civil wedding legalities

documents required

- Birth certificate
- Proof of single status for bride and groom
  in the form of a Statutory Declaration
- Divorce decree if divorced
- Death certificate of former spouse and
  original marriage certificate if widowed
- Legal proof if name has been changed
- Passport details for two witnesses
- All documentation must be original
- For full details of the marriage procedures,
  legalities, and documents required, contact
  the Cypriot Embassy or consulate in the
  state or city in which you reside

chapel of Limassol before he set off on
the third Crusade to the Holy Land.

It's romantic to drive through
sprawling banana and citrus plantations,
past sweeping bays where turtles nest,
and up winding mountain roads. There
are acres of vineyards as well as cedar,
cypress and white-blossomed almond
trees; juniper scents the air.

The InterContinental Aphrodite
Hills Resort Hotel is near Paphos,
overlooking the spot where Aphrodite,
the goddess of love, is said to have
emerged from the sea.

Set on 578 acres, the resort is an impeccable choice for weddings and honeymoons. The 290 elegant rooms and suites are done in colors to accentuate the sun's rays. Suites have their own private terrace or balcony where your own pool or Jacuzzi awaits.

For wining and dining there's a tempting choice of chic and relaxing bars, and both casual and informal restaurants. The elegant Leander Restaurant specializes in Euro-Asian cuisine, while The Mesogios provides an authentic Mediterranean dining experience.

The Retreat Spa offers a variety of relaxation and beauty treatments for bride and groom, including a Retreat Day so you can escape together for some well-earned tranquility and pampering.

The resort has its own onsite wedding coordinator and a choice of wedding packages.

You can celebrate your wedding in St. Catherine's Chapel, located at the heart of the resort. Beautifully decorated with hand-painted icons and religious artifacts, the chapel is just two minutes' walk from the hotel. Alternatively,

BRIDAL FILE

there's the contemporary setting of the clubhouse with its spectacular backdrop of the lake, the beach, gardens, or balcony.

You can even end your day with a firework display.

There are lots of romantic escapes around the area, but you should definitely take a trip to the Baths of Aphrodite where a tiny waterfall trickles into a deep green pool, hidden among shady trees. According to legend, Aphrodite bathed in these waters and it's said that if a woman takes a dip there, she will have eternal beauty. Not a bad start to married life!

LEFT

Spend your first night as husband and wife in the Presidential Suite.

———

BELOW LEFT

The InterContinental's Presidential Suite.

———

ABOVE

A romantic dinner for two by the pool.

- *Onsite wedding coordinator*
- *Wedding packages*
- *Weddings take place in St. Catherine's Chapel or the clubhouse*
- *Ceremony conducted by Town Hall official*
- *Transportation: horse-drawn carriage, vintage or open-top car, decorated Mercedes or limousine*
- *Music: folk singers and musicians, local choir, solo modern/classical singer, taped music, organ/piano, string trio or quartet*
- *Spa, gym, hair salon, beauty salon*
- *Hair stylist, beauty therapist, manicurist, masseur, makeup artist*
- *Photographer & videographer*
- *Individually designed cake*
- *Flowers & boutonnieres*
- *Floral table decorations*
- *Valet service*

LEFT

The Thermae at the Retreat Spa is a peaceful haven.

viva wyndham samaná
LAS TERRENAS
DOMINICAN REPUBLIC

"a plethora of pleasures"

Discover a special place where nature's treasures remain unspoiled and the simple joys of easy living can still be found. From verdant valleys and tropical rain forests to silky white beaches and perfect sunsets, the Dominican Republic has everything for a wedding in paradise. Explore the beauty of nature or the excitement of festivals, savor the many delights of fine cuisine, challenge yourself with exhilarating water sports, or just relax and enjoy the plethora of pleasures this tropical island offers.

BRIDAL FILE

- *Onsite wedding coordinator*
- *2 wedding packages*
- *Weddings take place in gazebo on beach or in one of the specialty restaurants*
- *Ceremony conducted by judge*
- *Music: DJ, local musicians playing folk music, solo singer*
- *Spa*
- *Photographer & videographer*
- *Individually designed cake*
- *Flowers*
- *Floral table decorations*
- *Separate room for the bride and groom to prepare for the wedding*

External suppliers can be suggested for the following:

- *Hair stylist, beauty therapist, manicurist, masseur, makeup artist*

It's easy to see why the Dominican Republic is the ideal setting for a memorable wedding and honeymoon.

Set in the heart of the Caribbean, its 805-mile coastline has some of the most beautiful beaches imaginable, cooled by tropical breezes and stretching as far as the eye can see.

Santo Domingo, a World Heritage Site, is a capital city with irresistible charm. In the old part of the city you'll find restored 16th-century buildings, open-air cafés, cosmopolitan restaurants, and spacious squares near the waterfront.

You realize just how old the city is when you visit the Basilica Menor de Santa Maria, Primada de America— the first cathedral to be founded by Christopher Columbus's son in 1514.

ABOVE

Spend lazy days lounging by the pool.

———

FAR LEFT

A short stroll to the sea through the tropical gardens.

RIGHT

Rooms or villas reflect the Caribbean style, and most have private balconies or terraces.

———

BELOW

Make time to explore the island's spectacular scenery.

All across the Dominican Republic are similarly intriguing sights, such as Altos de Chavon—a replica of a small medieval city built from coral bricks—and the beautiful and bohemian city of Las Terrenas, a town with unpaved streets.

On the northeast coast of the Dominican Republic near Las Terrenas is Viva Wyndham Samaná. Nestled on a beautiful golden sandy beach, surrounded by tropical splendor and easy elegance, the Viva Wyndham Samaná is the ideal place for a dream wedding and honeymoon.

The resort's elegantly appointed exteriors and interiors reflect the Caribbean-style architecture and design found throughout the island. Most of the 218 rooms and villas feature a private balcony and garden or ocean view.

Samaná offers three restaurants, each with its own menu and atmosphere.

The Mediterraneo specializes in Italian and Mediterranean dishes, as you would expect; visit Bambu restaurant for an Asian twist; or Cacao with its buffet-style service for casual dining.

The beachfront setting of the resort makes it the ultimate place to relax before your big day. Lounge on your private balcony, on terraces with breathtaking views of the ocean, unwind by the freshwater, outdoor pool, or enjoy a couple's massage in the spa.

Weddings at Viva Wyndham Samaná take place in an oceanfront gazebo on the beach with an amazing backdrop of lush vegetation, or in one of the specialty restaurants.

There's an onsite wedding coordinator and the resort offers two wedding packages. Ceremonies are conducted in Spanish by a judge and the package includes translation of the ceremony into English.

VITAL STATISTICS

rooms/villas 218 rooms/villas

email viva.samana@vivaresorts.com

website www.vivawyndhamresorts.com

legal requirements

- Couples need to be resident 3 working days prior to the ceremony
- The Dominican Republic does not require a marriage license but you need to register your ceremony with the Oficialia del Estado Civil
- After the wedding you will be given a document to prove that the wedding took place, but you need to request a marriage certificate from the local Justice of the Peace. This document is a valid marriage certificate

documents required

- Passport (original and copy)
- Birth certificate
- Single status affidavit translated into Spanish by an official translator
- Divorce decree translated into Spanish by an official translator
- Sealed legal transcripts of the birth certificate, single status affidavit and divorce certificates need to be prepared at the Dominican Consulate in the country where the documents were issued

After the ceremony you can indulge in a romantic dinner for two on the beach, and for pure pampering your breakfast will be served to you in the privacy of your own love nest the morning after the wedding.

During your stay there are plenty of activities and entertainments to enjoy, including beach games, water aerobics, windsurfing, sailing, scuba diving, volleyball, dance classes, and Spanish lessons. In the evening there are exciting theme parties and dancing at the resort's disco.

For adventures farther afield you can go horseback riding or take a 4WD through the mountains, visit the coastal mangrove swamps and rain forest, explore the area's many caves, or just perfect your tan on one of the peninsula's many secluded beaches.

ABOVE

A secluded beach—the perfect place for a romantic interlude.

outrigger on the lagoon
VITI LEVU
FIJI

"beautiful and seductive"

Discover Fiji, a group of islands that are out of this world. If you don't want to be disturbed, just hang a coconut shell on your door—it's a quaint old custom and just one many things that will make a wedding or honeymoon here memorable. However, there's very little to disturb your peace on any one of the Fijian islands that nestle in the sensational South Pacific.

Although it's more than 50 years since the musical *South Pacific* hit cinema screens, the image of this part of the world is still as beautiful and seductive as it was then.

With its 330 magical and exotic islands, Fiji has a unique, unspoiled, tranquil environment, and a fascinating blend of ancient cultures. Add to this the miles of coral reefs, amazing underwater experiences, and the seemingly endless variety of flora that covers the island, and you have the perfect place for an island wedding.

Often called the "Crossroads of the South Pacific" because of its location, Fiji enjoys a mild tropical climate tempered by sea breezes. From May to November the southeast trade winds blow, wafting the smell of the native frangipani plant around the islands and bringing the temperature down to 75°F.

ABOVE
Soak up some sunshine by one of the largest pools in the South Pacific.

—

LEFT
Experience award-winning cuisine at one of many venues and enjoy live entertainment at the Vakavanua Bar.

Viti Levu is the largest and oldest island in the archipelago. It's here, set amid a glorious landscape on the Coral Coast, that you find the Outrigger on the Lagoon.

The resort's 40 acres are landscaped with lush, fragrant, tropical gardens. Reminiscent of a Fijian village, it has 207 rooms and 47 *bures* (bungalows), all air-conditioned and with beachfront or resort views. The thatched bures have vaulted ceilings lined with exquisite hand-painted *masi* bark cloth. The deluxe rooms and bures have their own butler service, which includes the delivery of champagne and canapés every afternoon.

The resort has a wedding coordinator and a choice of wedding

VITAL STATISTICS

rooms 207 rooms/suites; 47 *bures* (bungalows)

email reservations@outrigger.com

website www.outrigger.com

legal requirements & documents required

- Valid passport (minimum validity of three months remaining) with valid visitor's permit
- Original or certified copy of birth certificate
- Divorce decree if divorced
- Death certificate of former spouse if widowed
- Officially witnessed consent of father if under 21 (or mother if father is deceased)
- Names and presence of two witnesses over 21
- Application forms for license from Head Office of Registrar of Births, Deaths, and Marriages in Suva or Divisional Registrar in Lautoka or Labasa, or any of the District Offices in Fiji
- License valid 28 days from date of issue
- Residency 6 working days, not necessarily before wedding but for entire stay. License obtained with single status confirmation on arrival on production of documents. Normally license obtained en route to chosen hotel or island

packages. For your ceremony, choose from a fragrant garden setting, the beach beneath swaying palms with a backdrop of the crystal clear South Pacific Ocean, or the Wedding Chapel set on a hilltop with magnificent views.

Arrangements can also be made for the couple to have a Fijian warrior escort, rent traditional Fijian costumes for the ceremony, or be serenaded by local musicians playing traditional wedding songs.

For pure indulgence, helicopter transfers can be arranged to the sister resort, Castaway Island, for a couple of extra-special honeymoon nights.

Evenings in Fiji are like nowhere else. Sip a sunset cocktail in the tropical garden Takia Bar before a candlelight dinner in the plantation-style setting of the Ivi Restaurant. If you prefer casual dining, then try the Vale Ni Kana Restaurant, where strolling local musicians will serenade you.

BRIDAL FILE

- *Onsite wedding coordinator*
- *2 wedding packages*
- *Weddings take place in Wedding Chapel, garden, or on beach*
- *Ceremonies conducted by church minister or wedding celebrant*
- *Music: Fijian serenaders, local church choir, taped music*
- *Spa & gym*
- *Hair salon, beauty salon, makeup artist*
- *Photographer & videographer*
- *Individually designed cake*
- *Flowers & boutonnieres*
- *Floral table decorations*
- *Separate rooms for bride and groom to prepare for wedding*
- *Valet service*

ABOVE

Watch the sun sink into the ocean as you indulge in a cocktail on the open-air deck of the Sundowner Bar.

———

FAR LEFT

Arrive in style through the impressive porte cochere.

———

LEFT

Want for nothing in the luxurious thatched-roof *bure* accommodation, complete with vaulted ceilings.

But for a true taste of Fiji, sample a buffet of local dishes, accompanied by traditional songs and dances performed at the twice-weekly Meke and Lovo—a Fijian dance and feast.

If you can tear yourself away from the resort, the capital, Suva, is colorful and fascinating with a rich colonial past. The Fijian Cultural Center at Pacific Harbor enables you to step into a warrior's raft for a history lesson with a difference, while a day cruise to sand-fringed Tivua Island is the ideal opportunity to enjoy a barbecue lunch and just chill out under the tropical sun.

princeville resort
KAUAI
HAWAII

"the perfect escape"

Cascading waterfalls, rainbows arching over emerald cliffs, and graceful hula dancers—Hawaii is the wedding destination of your dreams. The islands of Aloha are bursting with color and culture, and are set among some of the world's most breathtaking scenery. Relax on a palm-fringed beach, surf its waves, trek its mountains, dive with dolphins, kayak through rain forests, cruise the crystal waters, cycle up or ski down a volcano, or get pampered in a luxury spa on this idyllic archipelago.

TOP RIGHT

The elegant interior of a spacious Executive Suite.

—

BOTTOM RIGHT

Cafe Hanalei with its stunning view across the bay.

FAR RIGHT

The white sands of Kauai Beach.

ABOVE

The Makana Terrace—one of the beautiful wedding venues.

Rich in history, heritage, and culture, few destinations can offer Hawaii's combination of lush rain forests, active volcanoes, cliffs, snow-capped mountains, valleys, and sandy beaches with turquoise waters and coral reefs.

Hawaii, the most isolated land mass in the world, makes the perfect escape for weddings and honeymoons. Each of its six main islands is unique, making this a great place to enjoy island hopping.

Kauai, known as the Garden Isle, is the oldest and the lushest of the islands. Formed by a huge volcano, it's known for its remarkable, spectacular, and widely

varied landscape, from the desertlike Waimea Canyon, the "Grand Canyon of the Pacific," to the velvety green Na Pali Coast with its rugged cliffs.

On this island is Princeville Resort, described as "a resort like no other." Here sun-drenched days melt into soft,

candlelight nights. Serenity and the fragrance of exotic flowers lend still more romance to this romantic resort.

The 252 spacious rooms and suites have mountain or ocean views over Hanalei Bay. Rooms are done in the colors of the Hawaiian rain forests and have custom-designed furnishings and original artwork. The marble bathrooms feature oversize tubs, and there's even a magic window that brings the views of the ocean right into your room, then turns opaque for privacy.

VITAL STATISTICS

rooms 252 rooms/suites

website www.
princevillehotelhawaii.com

legal requirements

- The prospective bride
  and groom must appear
  together in person before
  a marriage license agent
  to apply for a license.
  Proxies are not allowed.
  Upon approval, marriage
  license issued at time
  application is made

documents required

- A valid I.D., e.g., passport

Princeville offers superb dining choices. La Cascata is a sophisticated fine-dining experience serving Mediterranean cuisine, while Cafe Hanalei is perfect for eating alfresco. Or you can sample the twice-weekly beachside Luau, a traditional feast with hula dancers and entertainment.

The health club and spa offer beauty and fitness programs including an island-style seaweed wrap or a couple's massage.

An infinity pool looks out to the sea and you can take surf lessons or enjoy other water activities at the beach.

The hotel has an onsite wedding coordinator and offers three wedding

BRIDAL FILE

- *Onsite wedding coordinator*
- *3 wedding packages*
- *Weddings take place on beach, Kamani Cove, Makana Terrace, or the Bay Terrace*
- *Ceremony conducted by denominational or nondenominational minister*
- *Music: local choir, solo classical singer, solo modern singer/duo, taped music, organ/piano, string trio/quartet, folk musicians/ singers, DJ, 10-piece band*
- *Spa, gym, hair salon, beauty salon*
- *Hair stylist, beauty therapist, manicurist, masseur, makeup artist*
- *Photographer & videographer*
- *Individually designed cake*
- *Flowers & boutonnieres*
- *Floral table decorations*
- *Separate room for the bride and groom to prepare for the wedding*
- *Valet service*

packages with 20 denominational and nondenominational celebrants available.

Say "I do" to the accompaniment of Hawaiian singers beside a white archway adorned with tropical flowers at one of the resort's four wedding locations—the beach, Kamani Cove, Makana Terrace, or the Bay Terrace.

To complete your special day there's a private romantic dinner, illuminated by the setting sun, soft candlelight, and glowing torches along the shore of Hanalei Bay, in a garden setting, or on the ocean-front terrace. For a touch of decadence you'll find chocolate-dipped strawberries and chilled champagne when you return to your room.

Though its tempting not to leave the resort, you may want to explore Kauai and all it has to offer. Take a Zodiac boat ride to the lush mountain ridges, travel by helicopter deep into the mountains, explore on horseback, or enjoy a sightseeing or shopping trip.

TOP

The hotel sits next to the turquoise South Pacific.

—

TOP LEFT

The Mediterranean-style La Cascata restaurant.

—

BOTTOM LEFT

The Na Pali cliffs offer a spectacular backdrop to the infinity pool.

round hill hotel
MONTEGO BAY
JAMAICA

"a dream wedding destination"

Jamaica is all you expect—glorious weather, superb beaches, reggae, rum, and unsurpassed scenic beauty. This island floats in the Caribbean just 18 degrees north of the Equator, and has acute variations in scenery, climate, and character, and is an Eden that lies buried under almost 3,000 species of plants and 252 species of tropical birds. With a potent mix of white sands, sparkling waterfalls, and majestic mountains, Jamaica is a dream wedding destination.

TOP RIGHT

The cool chic of one of the exclusive oceanfront rooms, designed by Ralph Lauren.

—

BELOW

The double infinity-edge pool faces the Caribbean Sea.

When Columbus first saw Jamaica in 1494, he is said to have declared that it was "the fairest isle that eyes ever beheld." Centuries later, when movie legend Errol Flynn's yacht washed up on the island after a hurricane, he wrote, "Never have I seen a land so beautiful," and promptly bought himself a villa there.

It's no secret that Jamaica has been having the same persuasive effect on people for centuries.

There's a sensuous atmosphere about this island, peppered with colorful sights and hypnotic rhythms, that keeps visitors coming back for more.

The first thing that strikes you when you arrive in Jamaica is the view of its dramatic hills rising through the mist of the sea—lush, green, and surrounded by sparkling turquoise-blue water.

Just a 25-minute drive from Montego Bay lies the legendary resort of Round Hill.

This exclusive property with its profuse gardens, secluded beaches, and world-class spa set in an 18th-century great house, has both privacy and timeless elegance—so it's easy to see why Round Hill is a favorite of celebrities and the wealthy.

The Pineapple House has 36 oceanfront rooms designed by Ralph Lauren. Luxuriously furnished with white stone floors and romantic four-poster mahogany bamboo beds, each room has breathtaking views overlooking the Caribbean Sea and the double infinity-edge pool.

There are also 27 privately owned villas surrounded by 30 acres of exotic tropical gardens that may be rented.

Each is beautifully decorated with plantation-style elegance and all face west, enjoying fabulous sunsets.

Days at Round Hill are casual and informal with the emphasis on relaxing and enjoying the facilities of this romantic retreat. Evenings, though not formal, are sophisticated and graceful. Dine alfresco under a starry sky on the seaside terrace or in the semi-enclosed Georgian Room—the menus in both restaurants are bound to tantalize the most discerning tastebuds.

At Round Hill every wedding is unique and special, with an onsite wedding coordinator who will personalize your own magical experience.

ABOVE
Aerial view of the resort and spa.

VITAL STATISTICS

rooms 36 oceanfront rooms in the Pineapple House, 27 privately owned villas to rent

email info@roundhilljamaica.com

website www.roundhilljamaica.com

legal requirements

- Couples can be married just 24 hours after arriving in Jamaica providing that a prior application has been made for a marriage license
- Applications for marriage licenses should be made to Ministry of National Security and Justice, 111 Harbour Street, Kingston

documents required

- Birth certificate
- Original divorce decree if divorced
- Certified copy of death certificate of former spouse if widowed

Ceremony settings range from private villas overlooking the sea to ocean terraces at sunset.

Couples can say "I do" to the sound of Jamaican music with a calypso, steel, or reggae band, while for the more conservative taste there's the choice of piano or violin accompaniment or a string trio.

Prior to the wedding, couples can enjoy a full range of pampering treatments in the spa, including a couple's massage. During the honeymoon the hotel offers special romantic gazebo dinners.

After the wedding there are plenty of tropical escapes to indulge in.

ABOVE

Plantation-style elegance in the Pineapple House.

—

TOP RIGHT

The pretty whitewashed entrance to the hotel.

—

RIGHT

Say "I do" surrounded by family and friends at a poolside ceremony.

BRIDAL FILE

- *Onsite wedding coordinator*
- *Weddings take place on sundeck, lawn, private beach, spa lawn, seaside terrace, Georgian Terrace, by the pool, in private villa, or Georgian Room*
- *Ceremony conducted by minister*
- *Music: string duo or trio, DJ, reggae, jazz, steel, or calypso band, steel solo drummer, piano, solo singer*
- *Spa, gym, hair salon, beauty salon*
- *Hair stylist, beauty therapist, manicurist, masseur, makeup artist*
- *Photographer & videographer*
- *Individually designed cake*
- *Flowers & boutonnieres*
- *Floral table decorations*
- *Separate room for bride and groom to prepare for wedding subject to availability*

Take a trip into the Blue Mountains National Park with its trails and magnificent views, visit Ocho Rios and walk through the warm cascading waters at the famous Dunn's River Falls, or enjoy a Black River Safari. See more of the island on horseback, take a bicycle tour, or marvel at the wonders of the deep in a modern semi-submarine.

one&only le saint géran
POSTE DE FLACQ
MAURITIUS

"the answer to every island-lover's dream"

Tropical breezes, no mass tourism, spectacular beaches—Mauritius is the answer to every island-lover's dream. Situated 1,200 miles off the southeastern coast of Africa just above the Tropic of Capricorn, the island is surrounded by a huge reef, sheltering shallow lagoons that meet a shoreline of sugar-white beaches. Away from the beaches there's a landscape of waterfall pools, sugarcane plains, and forests of ebony and eucalyptus, with ascending bare peaks of broken rocks that make a breathtaking moonscape of mountains.

No wonder Mark Twain declared that the magical island of Mauritius must have been the prototype for paradise—no charter flights, no pollution, and no high-rise development; in fact, it's every island-lover's idyll.

Mauritius has a worldwide reputation for the standard of its hotels, so if you are seeking a wedding and honeymoon filled with every conceivable luxury, this is the place for you. Its hotels are the epitome of sophistication, with gourmet food and superior nightlife at every turn.

On the golden peninsula of Belle Mare on the island's northeast coast is One&Only Le Saint Géran. Immortalized in Bernardin de Saint Pierre's novel *Paul et Virginie*, the resort's peninsula is near the site of Le Saint Géran shipwreck.

The hotel, set amid a garden of birdsong, cascades, and splashing fountains, has 60 acres of tropical gardens and thousands of swaying coconut trees. With the Indian Ocean on one side and a coral-sheltered lagoon on the other, it has more than a mile of secluded white sand beach.

Wherever you are at One&Only Le Saint Géran, the ocean is only steps

away—you can be splashing in the sea within a minute of getting out of bed.

The 149 suites and an exclusive private villa are extremely luxurious, with private terraces and balconies that look out toward the water.

The furnishings are tasteful and relaxing, with the Dutch and colonial influences pervading the elegant cane furniture, cool marble floors, and king-size beds with crisp Egyptian cotton sheets. For pure indulgence The Villa, hidden in a peaceful corner of the property, has a private pool and a team of valets, a butler, and its very own chef.

The jewel in Le Saint Géran's gastronomic crown is the gourmet restaurant, Spoon des Îles, perfect for that special intimate dinner. The La Terrasse restaurant offers an eclectic variety of local and international specialties, and there's entertainment to accompany dinner that provides an

ABOVE

The private villa has its own pool and dedicated staff to cater to your needs.

———

FAR LEFT

The Junior Suites feature a private terrace or balcony. All have 24-hour butler service.

———

LEFT

Sunset cocktails at the Paul & Virginie restaurant.

exquisite voyage of cultural discovery. Overlooking the Boathouse and green sugarcane-clad mountains, the Paul & Virginie restaurant serves pure and simple Mauritian dishes.

For pure pampering the hotel's exclusive Givenchy Spa is the last word in luxury, offering the very best in beauty, massage, and hair care. The fitness center has state-of-the-art equipment and a team of personal trainers.

BELOW
La Terrasse offers an eclectic menu with a mix of international and local cuisine.

VITAL STATISTICS

rooms 149 suites and private villa

email info@oneandonlylesaintgeran.com

website www.oneandonlyresorts.com

legal requirements & documents required

- Confirmation from hotel required for entry to Mauritius
- Couples must present original documents to Civil Status Officer in Port Louis, and together swear an affidavit at the Supreme Court
- After this the couple will be taken to the Civil Status Office for the publication of banns
- The civil marriage may take place 24 hours after the publication of banns, except on Saturday, Sunday, or public holidays

BRIDAL FILE

- *Onsite wedding coordinator*
- *Wedding package*
- *Weddings take place on the beach, the deck at the Paul & Virginie restaurant, or in the private villa*
- *Ceremony conducted by Civil Status Officer*
- *Transportation: horse-drawn carriage, catamaran, boat, horseback*
- *Music: local musicians playing traditional music, local choir, solo classical/modern singer, organ, string trio/quartet, folk musicians/singers*
- *Spa, gym, hair salon, beauty salon*
- *Hair stylist, beauty therapist, manicurist, masseur, makeup artist*
- *Photographer & videographer*
- *Individually designed cake*
- *Flowers & boutonnieres*
- *Floral table decorations*
- *Separate room for the bride and groom to prepare for the wedding*
- *Valet service*

The One&Only Le Saint Géran is the ultimate place to tie the knot. Weddings take place on the beach, on the deck at the Paul & Virginie restaurant, or in the private villa. They are conducted by a Civil Status Officer and there's a wedding coordinator on site to help with your arrangements.

Following your ceremony you can take a ride in a horse and carriage along the coast or a boat trip on the lagoon that will leave you with precious memories of your first moments together as man and wife. Later a dinner beneath the stars at the Paul & Virginie restaurant will end your day.

During your stay there are plenty of adventures to be had. Start the day with a romantic beach breakfast, followed by a splash in the warm blue waters of the lagoon. Discover fabulous waterfalls, reefs for snorkeling, or take one of the hotel's suggested day trips designed for individual exploration of the island.

ABOVE
The tranquil setting of the Boathouse.

———

BELOW
The opulent lobby.

taj exotica resort & spa
WOLMAR
MAURITIUS

"a fairytale island"

Mauritius is a fairytale island often referred to as the land of rainbows, waterfalls, and shooting stars. Rich in legend and steeped in exotic history, it's like a beautiful tropical garden floating in the Indian Ocean. Inland there are dramatic mountains, waterfalls, and nature parks, while the beauty of its beaches is merely a taste of the stunning marine wonderland that lies just below the surface of the waves. this piece of paradise is a fascinating melting pot of different cultures, full of different sights and traditions.

Mauritius is a fantastic wedding destination, offering just the right surroundings to begin your married life.

From soaring jungle-clad mountains to verdant country plains, serene temples with their own legends and lore, to picturesque colonial sugar plantations, there is so much to experience and enjoy on the island of Mauritius.

Stroll hand in hand on the edge of the sand and gaze out to the deep blue sea, soak up the sun under a swaying palm, or take a trip to the Ile aux Cerfs, with its miles and miles of deserted sands, and discover your very own Robinson Crusoe-style island.

The jewel in Mauritius's crown is its hotels. Most lead straight down to the beach through tropical gardens of ornamental palm trees, and they are renowned for their discreet luxury, privacy, and unobtrusive service.

Spread across 27 acres with a backdrop of majestic mountains and encircled by a lagoon, the Taj Exotica Resort & Spa at Wolmar Beach provides the perfect wedding destination.

LEFT

Bathrooms offer elegant simplicity.

BELOW

Each Presidential Suite has its own infinity pool and overlooks the ocean.

VITAL STATISTICS

rooms 65 villas with pool

email Exotica.mauritius@tajhotels.com

website www.tajhotels.com

legal requirements & documents required

- Couples must present original documents to Civil Status Officer in Port Louis, and together swear an affidavit at the Supreme Court
- After this the couple will be taken to the Civil Status Office for the publication of banns
- The civil marriage may take place 24 hours after the publication of banns, except on Saturday, Sunday, or public holidays

ABOVE

The Luxury Suites feature shaded sofa seating, set against the backdrop of an intimate patio courtyard.

——

TOP RIGHT

Take a dip after dark in your candlelight pool.

——

BOTTOM RIGHT

Each of the Taj Grande spa's six treatment suites has its own relaxation garden.

Overlooking the blue waters of Tamarin Bay, this all-villa resort, with its Mauritian architecture provides luxury, tranquility, and privacy.

Each of the 65 villas has breathtaking views, decor inspired by French colonial, Indian, African, and Arabic design, and comes with its own swimming pool, alfresco dining options, and personalized service.

The Presidential Suites are luxury personified with magnificent views of the ocean and the peak at Tamarin from every room. They have their own infinity pools, private patio gardens, and state-of-the-art marble bathrooms, plus a sun terrace with fan-cooled seating areas, and 24-hour butler service.

The hotel enjoys a reputation for its high standard of cuisine, whether it's a romantic dinner for two on your own terrace, casual alfresco dining in the Coast2Coast restaurant, or the ultimate dining experience in the Cilantro restaurant, sampling the finest Pan-Asian cuisine.

A wonderful array of treatments is available in the Taj Grande spa, which has its own yoga pavilion. Highly recommended for honeymooners is a candlelight aromatherapy massage with sensuous oils followed by a rose-petal bath and time alone in a cabana with a bottle of champagne, or you may prefer a massage in the privacy of your own villa.

BRIDAL FILE

- *Onsite wedding coordinator*
- *Wedding package*
- *Weddings take place on private jetty, beach, by the pool, in private villa, or under the Raj tent*
- *Ceremony conducted by celebrant*
- *Music: guitar, violin, saxophone, singer*
- *Spa, gym, beauty salon*
- *Hair stylist, beauty therapist, manicurist, masseur, makeup artist*
- *Photographer & videographer*
- *Individually designed cake*
- *Flowers & boutonnieres*
- *Floral table decorations*
- *Separate room provided for bride and groom to prepare for the wedding*
- *Valet service*

The resort's own wedding coordinator will help with the arrangements for your wedding, whether it's on the private jetty, beach, by the pool, in your villa, or under the Raj tent.

There's a good range of leisure facilities here, including a sports center and a large swimming pool, as well as an excellent choice of excursions. These include sunset cruises, and 4WD safaris, dolphin encounters, and an undersea walk.

Alternatively you can rent a car and visit Port Louis, the capital, with its kaleidoscope of sights, smells, sounds, and tastes. Small enough to explore on foot, it's a jumble of new and old buildings, mosques, churches, and temples, plus a fascinating old covered market.

The Pamplemousse Royal Botanical Gardens are ideal for a romantic stroll, with their astonishing array of rare indigenous plants, trees, and endangered species. But for a truly tranquil experience, visit the sacred lake of Grand Bassin. Surrounded by forests, with shrines and a small temple, legend has it that the lake contains nocturnal fairies.

montpelier plantation inn
MONTPELIER
NEVIS

"a truly romantic sanctuary"

Imagine a romantic getaway where quaint old Caribbean charm reigns supreme. Rain forest tumbles down the slopes of Nevis Peak to tranquil, palm-fringed white sand beaches lapped by inviting warm tropical waters. There's not a high-rise beach resort in sight, just beautifully restored plantation houses, fields of sugarcane waving gracefully in the warm breeze, and lush island paths ideal for romantic walks, making this piece of paradise the ultimate wedding and honeymoon destination.

VITAL STATISTICS

rooms 17 rooms/suites

email

info@montpeliernevis.com

website

www.montpeliernevis.com

legal requirements

- Couples must be resident on Nevis for a minimum of 3 working days before the wedding
- Couples must be at the resident magistrate's office the day after arrival to complete forms and present documents

documents required

- Birth certificate
- Valid passport
- Return tickets to country of residence
- If single, an affidavit to confirm single status. If divorced, original divorce decree. If widowed, original marriage certificate, plus spouse's death certificate
- Legal proof if name has been changed

LEFT

The historic Sugar Mill commands a poolside view.

———

TOP RIGHT

The shaded Plantation Inn.

———

MIDDLE

Cool interiors are decorated with tropical flowers.

Nevis looks just like a tropical island should. Part of the Leeward Islands, it is 230 miles southeast of Puerto Rico and less than 2 miles southeast of its sister island, St. Kitts. This island is only 7 miles long and 5 miles wide, with lush vegetation rising to the peak of Mount Nevis.

One of the Caribbean's best-kept secrets, the island of Nevis is for those who are seeking a truly romantic sanctuary amid a laid-back, peaceful, and luxurious setting.

You can drive around the island in one day and see most of the main sights in an afternoon.

Charleston, the capital, has a handful of shops and a waterfront market. There are tiny churches like the Fig Tree Church, set in a tropical garden, and plantation houses that look like gingerbread cottages, most of which are now hotels.

The Montpelier Plantation Inn, surrounded by over 60 acres of unspoiled mountainside and set 750 feet above sea level, is an idyllic wedding and honeymoon haven. During the 18th century it was a working sugar plantation and witness to the marriage of Lord Nelson to Fanny Nisbet in 1787.

Today both the plantation and inn have been meticulously restored to their former glory in keeping with their heritage of elegance and style.

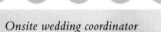

BRIDAL FILE

- *Onsite wedding coordinator*
- *Wedding package*
- *Weddings take place in the 18th-century Sugar Mill, in the Great Room, on the private beach, in the gardens, or under the 200-year-old tree where Lord Nelson was married*
- *Ceremony conducted by minister, priest, or magistrate*
- *Music: local musicians playing traditional music, local choir, solo classical/modern singer, taped music, organ/piano, calypso band*
- *Gym arranged locally*
- *Hair stylist can be arranged to come to hotel*
- *Beauty therapist, manicurist, masseur*
- *Photographer*
- *Individually designed cake*
- *Flowers & boutonnieres*
- *Floral table decorations*
- *Separate room for the bride and groom to prepare for the wedding subject to availability*

Walk through the tropical gardens, relax in a hammock, or find a quiet spot on the inn's private beach, a pretty two-acre section of Pinney's Beach on the calm west coast of Nevis. The manicured lawns and soft beach are dotted with gazebos and lounge chairs. The beach has a pavilion for barbecue lunches, and there's a regular shuttle service from the hotel to the beach.

The 17 cottage-style guest rooms sit under towering palms in bird-filled gardens. Decorated in luxurious but simple style, each room has a view of the ocean, while private verandas capture the warmth of the sun, the gentle breezes, and the fresh mountain air.

In the evening, retreat to the comfort of the Great Room for drinks and canapés; then dine by candlelight overlooking the lights of Charlestown and St. Kitts.

RIGHT

The tropical sky reflected in the sparking water of the Mosaic Pool.

—

BELOW RIGHT

Relax in the lush gardens.

—

BELOW

Dine on the terrace amid exotic plants and flowers.

But for pure indulgence, experience intimate candlelight dining in the 18th-century sugar mill, which serves only 12 people at a time.

Holding your wedding at Montpelier is like having it in your own Caribbean country house, except there's a wedding coordinator onsite to take care of all the details.

Make your vows in the Great Room, in the grounds, around the gardens, on the private beach, or inside the historic Sugar Mill. You can even choose the spot where Lord Nelson was married, under the 200-year-old ficus tree with its intertwined trunks and spreading branches.

After the ceremony take a romantic ride in a horse-drawn carriage, boat, luxury car, or even on horseback.

If you want to explore Nevis's beauty there are island ecologists on hand to guide you on hikes through the tropical rain forest and deserted sugar plantations. Alternatively, visit nearby St. Kitts, go mountain biking, or just enjoy a champagne picnic on a nearby island.

carrington resort
KAITAIA
NORTH ISLAND

"a captivating place for saying 'I do'"

Secluded beaches, snow-capped mountains, lush greenery, and some of the world's most stunning coastlines make the North Island of New Zealand a captivating place for saying "I do." Every inch of this island, a place of magnificent natural splendor, steeped in history and Maori culture, has something rich, rare, unique, and truly wonderful to offer. It's adventurous and dramatic, yet at the same time peaceful and tranquil, and provides the perfect balance between rest, indulgence, and adventure.

ABOVE
The lounge of a two-bedroom villa with its spectacular view.

The subtropical Northland of New Zealand promises visitors a contrast between the relative sophistication of the east coast and the soulful simplicity of the west coast. Much of its extensive coastline remains unspoiled, and it's an aquatic playground for adventure activities and escapist relaxation.

You can't escape the ocean in Northland—nor would you want to. Sail around the Bay of Islands, swim with dolphins, dive down to a wreck, or just snooze under the pohutukawa trees on its famous beaches.

Northland's history is as rich and interesting as its coast and rolling countryside. It's believed that the first Polynesian voyagers arrived here during the 11th century. Today Waitangi is the seat of Maori culture, which is still very much alive in this region. Europeans began to settle here in the 1840s, further enriching the region's past.

The Karikari Peninsula fronts Doubtless Bay on its southern side and the Pacific Ocean on the north. Renowned for its beautiful white sandy beaches, particularly Tokerau and Karikari, and its secluded coves, the jewel in its crown is Maitai Bay, one of the most beautiful and idyllic beaches in New Zealand.

The Carrington Resort is superbly situated on the magnificent Karikari Peninsula. Private, sumptuous, sophisticated, and a tailor-made for romantic weddings and blissful honeymoons, Carrington offers splendid isolation with five-star options.

It is set in the middle of the Carrington Farms Estate, a 3,000-acre ecologically planned property of secluded virgin beaches and restored natural wetlands in the warmest area of New Zealand closest to the equator. Carrington has moderate weather patterns similar to the coastal areas of southern California.

Luxury accommodation is provided in a choice of air-conditioned lodge or villa, with private verandas or porches looking out over the ocean or native bush and vineyard, and every modern amenity for your comfort.

ABOVE

A wedding amid unspoiled natural beauty.

——

MIDDLE

A view of the lodge at dusk.

RIGHT

Lodge rooms combine
stylish interiors with private
verandas and views of
the ocean.

—

BELOW

The outdoor heated infinity
pool.

TOP RIGHT

Early morning horseback
riding on the beach.

—

BOTTOM RIGHT

The natural beauty of
Maitai Bay.

VITAL STATISTICS

rooms 10 lodge rooms/14 villas

email info@carrington.co.nz

website www.carrington.co.nz

**legal requirements & documents
required**

- Residency 3 days before date of wedding
- Couples can complete most of the
  formalities before arriving in New
  Zealand
- The legalities are so complex it is
  recommended that you contact the
  New Zealand Embassy or the Consulate
  in your city or state for full information
  on the documents required and legal
  procedures for marrying in New Zealand

Carrington's restaurant offers superb
fine dining with a relaxed atmosphere
and breathtaking views. The varied
menus include a high ratio of locally
grown produce as well as fresh local
seafood and wines.

The resort provides a breathtakingly
beautiful backdrop for a wedding.

Marriages can take place anywhere
on the resort—overlooking the vineyards,
on the secluded beach, or in front of the
dining room with its stunning views.

The hotel has a wedding coordinator,
but couples need to arrange a celebrant
who will look after all the legalities.

After your specially created post-
nuptial dinner in the evening, you can
return to the privacy of your room.

BRIDAL FILE

There you'll find a bottle of local wine to sip under the stars on your veranda.

There is a plethora of things to do onsite at Carrington, ranging from golf, horseback riding, tennis, swimming in the heated pool, a gym, wine-tasting tours, boat excursions, canoeing, or picnics to some secluded cove. Alternatively, you can just unwind and appreciate the stunning natural landscapes of the subtropical Northland on New Zealand's North Island.

- *Onsite wedding coordinator*
- *Wedding packages*
- *Weddings take place anywhere on the resort*
- *Ceremony conducted by celebrant*
- *Transportation: vintage cars, limousines*
- *Music: local musicians playing traditional native music, solo classical/modern singer, taped music, organ/piano, string trio/quartet, folk music, DJ or modern band*
- *Spa, gym*
- *Separate room for the bride and groom to prepare for the wedding*
- *Valet service*

All the following services are provided by local salons/suppliers and are available on an "on-call" service to the hotel:

- *Hair stylist, beauty therapist, manicurist, masseur, makeup artist*
- *Photographer & videographer*
- *Individually designed cake*
- *Flowers & boutonnieres*
- *Floral table decorations*

labriz silhouette
SILHOUETTE ISLAND
SEYCHELLES

"a wedding in paradise"

Uncrowded, unspoiled, and unique, these mystical islands are literally a thousand miles from anywhere, making them the perfect wedding destination. More than 100 islands make up the Seychelles archipelago spread over 176 square miles of the Indian Ocean. Seychelles beaches rank among the best in the world. Silver-white sand stretches as far as the eye can see and beyond, and sun-lovers will revel in the even year-round temperature that rarely falls below 75° F.

RIGHT

Garden villas have outdoor showers with views of spectacular Mount Dauban.

——

BELOW

Enjoy a cool drink at the bar.

Discovered only two centuries ago and thought by many to be the original Garden of Eden, the Seychelles are some of the most beautiful and romantic islands in the world.

The main island, Mahé, is only 17 miles long. It's a spectacular place with huge mountains as its backbone, and tropical vegetation that gives it a wild feeling.

Mahé, with its international airport, is the economic and political center of the Seychelles, but there are also 70 beaches scattered around the island.

Island-hopping is the best way to appreciate all these small places have to offer, because each is very different. From Praslin with its lush interior and tranquil Vallée de Mai, the only place in the world where you'll find the legendary Coco de Mer, the fruit from an exclusive palm tree with supposed aphrodisiac powers—to the tiny Robinson Crusoe-style island of Moyenne, each has its own individuality.

Silhouette Island is a 45-minute boat trip or 15-minute helicopter transfer away from Mahé. It's an amazing place where mountains tower overhead, their peaks seemingly touching the clouds, while the rain forests sweep down to meet the white sands.

Set on a one-mile, powder-white beach is Labriz Silhouette, the only hotel on the island. This idyllic property is tailor-made for a wedding in paradise.

Accommodation at Labriz is luxurious. There are 17 two-roomed pavilions with their own pool, private garden, bathroom with a tub for two, and a separate pavilion for enjoying a spa treatment or a romantic dinner.

ABOVE

Wake up to an ocean view from your beach villa.

———

BELOW LEFT

Aerial view of the resort.

The 63 beach villas are steps away from the ocean, some with their own plunge pool, while the 30 garden villas are set amid the lush greenery with spectacular views.

The mountainside treatment suites of the resort's Aquum Spa nestle amid exotic vegetation and massive granite boulders, with a yoga pavilion perched at the top of a giant rock to welcome the morning sun. It's here you can enjoy an intuitive touch massage and an aroma waves facial for two on your wedding morning.

Dining options at Labriz include the fabulous Sakura, set right on the beach, the Portobello with views of Mount Dauban, and Grann Kaz, the restored plantation home of the previous owners of the island.

Labriz Silhouette offers a wedding package and a dedicated onsite wedding coordinator.

VITAL STATISTICS

rooms 17 pavilions, 63 beach villas, 30 garden villas

email labrizsilhouette@slh.com

website www.slh.com/labrizsilhouette

legal requirements

- 3-day residency in the Seychelles is required by law prior to the wedding.
- An apostille (a special letter and stamp) is required to validate the marriage certificate obtained after the civil ceremony for all nationalities except British nationals. This stamp is available from the Registrar's Office located at the Supreme Court in Victoria, Mahé

documents required

- Birth certificate
- Passport
- Legal proof if name has been changed
- Divorce decree if divorced
- Death certificate of former spouse and marriage certificate if widowed

Weddings take place on the beach, which is decorated for the occasion, or on the terrace. After cutting the cake there's a sunset cruise followed by a specially created four-course dinner in the restaurant. When you return to your villa, you'll find your bed decorated and the tub filled with rose petals and exotic essential oils.

Labriz offers tennis, diving, and nonmotorized water sports. And if you want to explore the nature and culture of the Seychelles, beach barbecue excursions, mountain walks, excursions to Mahé, or island-hopping trips can be arranged.

ABOVE

Relax together in the Aquum Spa hot tub.

BRIDAL FILE

- Onsite wedding coordinator
- Wedding package
- Weddings take place on beach or terrace
- Ceremony conducted by official registrar from Mahé
- Transportaion: vintage cars, limousines
- Music: local Creole music played by duo
- Spa, gym, beauty salon
- Beauty therapist, manicurist, masseur
- Hairstylist, make-up artist available from Mahé
- Photographer & videographer available from Mahé
- Individually designed cake
- Flowers
- Floral table decorations
- Separate room for the bride and groom to prepare for the wedding
- Valet service

lesport
CAP ESTATE
ST. LUCIA

"the freedom to do it your way"

St. Lucia's natural beauty could have been created for romantics, with its palm-fringed beaches, elegant old plantation houses, soft tropical air, and hypnotic steel-band music. It's no wonder that getting married in St. Lucia is referred to by locals as a "marriage made in heaven." From a barefoot wedding on a deserted beach to saying "I do" at the base of a gorgeous waterfall, in a plantation house, a magical rain forest, or even underwater, the island offers you the freedom to do it your way.

St. Lucia is the quintessential tropical island paradise. This eastern Caribbean island offers unrivaled beauty and romance. Rugged mountain peaks rise majestically from the sea, waterfalls cascade through the luscious rain forests, and colorful marine life shimmers from beneath turquoise waves.

The Atlantic Ocean rims St. Lucia's eastern shore while the Caribbean Sea lines the west coast, offering calm surf and fine beaches.

The interior of possibly the greenest island in the Caribbean is tropical, lush, and vibrant with color. Banana, coconut, mango, and papaya trees grow in profusion, and wild orchids, giant ferns, and birds of paradise flourish among the mineral baths and waterfalls.

Tucked into its own attractive cove at the northern tip of St. Lucia is LeSport, a large upbeat resort and one of the finest all-inclusive hotels in the Caribbean.

But LeSport is more than just a resort. Not only does it offer a huge range of sports and activities, but also personalized programs of relaxation, therapies, and treatments in The Oasis spa, a Moorish-style palace. The spa has been rated number one in the world and offers the ultimate choice in therapies. Pre-wedding treatments include an exotic jasmine flower bath and Balinese massage. There's even a honeymoon massage, and a couple's session where you can learn a few tips for when you return home.

VITAL STATISTICS

rooms 155 rooms/suites with ocean or

garden views

email lesport@thebodyholiday.com

website www.thebodyholiday.com

legal requirements

- Marriages can take place after a minimum of 3 working days on the island
- Legal offices on the island only operate Monday to Friday, so weddings cannot be conducted on weekends and public holidays

documents required

- Passport
- Airport immigration form
- Birth certificate
- Divorce decree if divorced
- Death certificate of former spouse if widowed
- Legal proof if name has been changed

The 155 rooms at LeSport have either ocean or tropical garden views. The rooms are decorated with rare hummingbird prints, pastel-colored fabrics and draped king-size beds. Some have French doors that lead out onto private balconies. There's no better place to sip champagne and watch the sun go down.

Every hot place has a hot bar. At LeSport it's the Piano Bar with its elegant and sophisticated ambience. The resort is famed for its Tao Restaurant, named by *Conde Nast Traveler* as one of the 60 "hot tables" in the world, perfect for a romantic dinner.

ABOVE

Spend your nights in rich Caribbean colonial-inspired decor.

———

FAR LEFT

The Anse la Ray waterfall nestles amid lush vegetation.

LEFT

Discover the intense pleasure of body rejuvenation at the Oasis Spa.

BRIDAL FILE

- *Onsite wedding coordinator*
- *4 wedding packages*
- *Weddings take place in a number of venues, including beachside gazebo, wedding chapel, garden*
- *Ceremonies conducted by celebrant*
- *Music: steel band, guitarist, saxophonist*
- *Spa, gym, hair salon, beauty salon*
- *Hair stylist, beauty therapist, manicurist, masseur, makeup artist*
- *Photographer & videographer*
- *Individually designed cake*
- *Flowers & boutonnieres*
- *Floral table decorations*

If you prefer dining within the sight and sound of the sea, as well as within earshot, the Cariblue is for you.

One of the main reasons many couples choose LeSport for their wedding is that it is not a "wedding factory." With the onsite wedding coordinator offering a more customized personal approach to each couple, ceremonies can take place in the shade of a gingerbread oceanfront gazebo decorated with tropical flowers, with a steel band providing the music. Later you can celebrate your marriage with a romantic beach dinner with butler service.

LeSport offers lots of activities, but it's worth taking some time to explore the island. Visit the capital, Castries, to soak up some of the atmosphere, then book a day trip to the rain forest for some trekking or the Diamond Falls for a mineral bath. All will set the perfect scene for the beginning of your lives together.

ABOVE

Sample eight different kinds of massage from Swedish to the exotic Ayurvedic.

——

FAR LEFT

A view across the pool to the pristine beach.

sheraton grande laguna
PHUKET
THAILAND

"heaven on earth"

Thailand is a country simmering with romance. Exotic and alluring, it's a beautiful tropical paradise, a breathtaking nirvana that lovers will instantly call home. Blessed with diversity and variety, this ancient mystical land has it all—palm-studded white sandy beaches, forested mountains cloaked in dawn mists, well-preserved ruins of historic civilizations, and a vibrant exciting capital, Bangkok, where old and new blend beautifully in dramatic fashion.

ABOVE

Retreat to a space that is spacious, elegant, and filled with opulence.

Nestled in the heart of Southeast Asia, Thailand is known as the gateway to Asia. Its pleasant year-round climate, arresting scenery, and remarkable architecture are famous, and its welcoming people and rich, exuberant culture are equally fascinating.

Some 540 miles south of Bangkok, Phuket is Thailand's largest island, and is shaped like an irregular pearl measuring approximately 13 miles at its longest. It's connected to the mainland by a causeway and has a coastline fringed with white sandy beaches and quiet coves, bathed by the clear blue water of the Andaman Sea with a background of green hills, coconut groves, and rubber plantations.

Set against a dazzling backdrop of bright white sand and sparkling indigo lagoons is Sheraton Grande Laguna, ranked among the five best resorts in Asia-Pacific. This piece of paradise, providing optimum service and luxury, is the ultimate wedding venue.

The 411 beautifully appointed guest rooms and villas are luxurious and spacious, with a touch of elegant opulence reflecting the country's exotic culture.

VITAL STATISTICS

rooms 411 rooms/villas

email sheratonphuket@
luxurycollection.com

website www.luxurycollection.
com/phuket

legal requirements & documents required

- Allow 4–6 working days prior to the wedding to complete legal documentation
- Marriage in Thailand should be performed according to Thai law
- A religious ceremony alone is not legally binding and your marriage must be registered at the nearest Amphoe (District) Office. Arrange for an official to attend your ceremony
- You must be aged at least 18 years and not divorced for fewer than 310 days
- If either party is widowed or divorced, relevant paperwork must be provided and translated into Thai
- You will require an affirmation of freedom to marry which should be translated into Thai
- Your marriage certificate will be in Thai. It is recommended that you commission a "sworn translation" of the marriage certificate from a translation bureau for legal use
- Passports must be valid for at least 6 months from the date of entry to Thailand

ABOVE

Say your vows in the Wedding Chapel overlooking the lagoon.

BRIDAL FILE
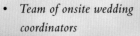

- *Team of onsite wedding coordinators*
- *2 wedding packages*
- *Weddings take place in the Wedding Chapel, private gardens, on the beach*
- *Ceremony conducted by celebrant, priest, or Thai monk*
- *Transportation: vintage cars, limousines*
- *Music: local musicians playing traditional music, solo modern singer, taped music, organ/piano, string trio/quartet, folk musicians and singer*
- *Spa, gym, hair salon, beauty salon*
- *Hair stylist, beauty therapist, manicurist, masseur, makeup artist*
- *Photographer & videographer*
- *Individually designed cake*
- *Flowers & boutonnieres*
- *Floral table decorations*
- *Separate room for the bride and groom to prepare for the wedding*
- *Valet service*

The one-bedroom Lagoon Villas are totally romantic. They are connected to the resort via a series of bridges with views of the tranquil lagoon. Each two-story villa features contemporary interior decor, a loft-style bedroom, open-air shower with sunken Jacuzzi, and a large, lower-level balcony connected to a private jetty for check-in by boat.

The Sheraton Grande Laguna is a culinary haven of excellence with 10 dining venues featuring gourmet, Thai favorites, Chinese spa cuisine, Italian, and Asian specialties, all served while guests enjoy the air-conditioned comfort or the tropical breeze outside.

Couples can take time out to pamper body and soul at the Angsana Spa with its unique and traditional spa treatments. For the more active there are water sports, a fitness center, or swimming in Asia's longest freshwater pool, with two Jacuzzis and waterfall features, which winds its way through the main hotel buildings.

Depending on the style of your wedding, the service will be conducted by a celebrant, priest, or Thai monk.

Following your marriage you can be greeted by a baby elephant or have Chiang Mai lanterns released. In the evening enjoy a romantic barbecue dinner either in your villa or on the beach, or even a sunset elephant ride.

FAR LEFT
The two-story Lagoon Villas are built on stilts over the water.

———

BOTTOM LEFT
The living accommodation in one of the luxury Lagoon Villas.

———

LEFT
Dine under an illuminated canopy after your wedding.

———

BELOW
Enjoy a romantic lunch for two in a boat on the lagoon.

The resort has a team of wedding coordinators and offers two wedding packages. Before the ceremony, couples need to visit Bangkok to complete the legal formalities, and the wedding coordinators are happy to assist.

There is a choice of places within the resort to hold ceremonies—the Laguna's own Wedding Chapel, the beach, or private gardens with glorious views.

During your honeymoon there are plenty of activities and adventures to choose from, including bungee-jumping, bike tours, private speedboat excursions, Thai and Italian cooking classes, or even a lagoon feast for two, experiencing authentic Thai food as you cruise the tranquil lagoon.

wyndham sugar bay resort & spa
ST. THOMAS
U.S. VIRGIN ISLANDS

"an exquisitely exotic experience"

Powder-white sand beaches, crystal clear waters, and colorful towns—the U.S. Virgin Islands are the stuff of dreams. Walk down an aisle framed by seashells, say your vows on a hilltop, promise yourselves to each other in the fragrant air of a tropical garden, or toss your bouquet into a tranquil harbor at sunset. Whatever fantasy you envisage for your special day, on these magical islands it will be an exquisitely exotic experience.

In 1917, the United States paid $25 million to Denmark in exchange for the group of Caribbean islands now known as the U.S. Virgin Islands. While this was more than the U.S. had ever spent before to acquire land, in hindsight there's no doubt it was a spectacular bargain.

Known affectionately as America's Caribbean, the 50 U.S. Virgin Islands enjoy an all-year-round warm climate. Some are rocks or islets set in shimmering turquoise waters, while the three major islands are St. Croix, St. John, and St. Thomas, each distinguished by its own personality.

The liveliest of the islands is St. Thomas, with its rich cultural and cosmopolitan atmosphere. The bustling harbor town of Charlotte Amalie is full of fine restaurants, historic monuments, and warehouse shops, and has an invigorating nightlife.

RIGHT

Tuscany's restaurant features elegant trompe l'oeil and wood panelling.

———

BELOW

The spectacular setting of St. John Terrace.

The picturesque Magens Bay has been voted one of the most beautiful beaches in the world.

Carved into a mountainside on the northeast end of St. Thomas is Wyndham Sugar Bay Resort & Spa. With breathtaking mountain and ocean views, and its very own secluded, white-sand beach, it's a wonderful wedding destination.

Cooling Caribbean breezes welcome you to this all-inclusive resort with 301 guest rooms and suites, all with spectacular views. The Caribbean-style rooms are full of delightful touches, including colonial-style furniture, ceiling fans, private balconies, and marble bathrooms.

Journeys Spa, voted the best spa in the Virgin Islands, is the perfect place to experience some pre-wedding pampering. Surrounded by exotic tropical plants, it's a special retreat where you can reflect and relax in peace and tranquility, and indulge in an extensive array of spa treatments and services, including a couple's massage.

BRIDAL FILE

- *Onsite wedding coordinator*
- *3 wedding packages*
- *Weddings take place on beach, or on St. John Terrace*
- *Ceremony conducted by nondenominational minister*
- *Transportation: vintage cars, limousines*
- *Music: DJ, classical guitar/violin reggae, calypso, rock, and steel drum bands*
- *Spa, gym, beauty salon*
- *Beauty therapist, manicurist, masseur*
- *Photographer & videographer*
- *Individually designed cake*
- *Flowers & boutonnieres*
- *Floral table decorations*

VITAL STATISTICS

rooms 301 rooms/suites

website www.wyndham.com

legal requirements & documents required

- You must complete a marriage applicationand submit it to the Superior Court of the U.S.V.I. one month prior to the ceremony date. Inform the court of the date you intend to pick up the license

- Previous marriages: if widowed, certified copy of death of spouse certificate must accompany application; if divorced, the divorce must be final 30 days prior to the application date. The decree must show a raised stamp or seal. It must be the original certified copy

- Make copies of the information you send to the court, and take them with you to St. Thomas. Send to: Superior Court of Virgin Islands, 5400 Veterans Drive, St. Thomas, USVI 00802

- Once in St. Thomas you will need to pick up your license at the Superior Court in downtown Charlotte Amalie. It's open all day Monday to Friday and Saturday from 10.00 to noon. Closed on holidays. There are 20 holidays in St. Thomas so check with your wedding coordinator that your dates are not in conflict with these

And when the sun goes down, there's a large number of excellent restaurants to savor, from the fine dining of Tuscany's, the intimate candlelight atmosphere of The Manor House, to the contemporary, casual bistro feel of the poolside Mangrove Restaurant.

Wyndham Sugar Bay Resort offers three wedding packages and the services of an onsite wedding coordinator.

ABOVE

Private balconies overlook the three pools and have superb mountain and ocean views.

———

ABOVE RIGHT

A view along the resort's beach.

———

RIGHT

The sweeping staircase of the resort's elegant lobby.

———

LEFT

Enjoy a sunset massage from Journeys Spa.

There are two breathtaking locations for saying "I do" at the resort. You can choose the St. John Terrace, suspended 100 feet above water, with spectacular views of the islands and a gleaming white gazebo, or you may prefer an intimate romantic ceremony on the beach with swaying palm trees and your feet in the sand.

In addition you might like to take a page from the islands' rich and colorful history and incorporate authentic music and traditions into the ceremony. One such custom is "Jumping the Broom."

This is a centuries-old wedding ritual of African origin that signifies the joining of two families. Other customs include traditional steel drum music and "Black Cake," a rum-cured cake that is given to guests as a parting favor.

There's plenty to see and do around the island if you can tear yourself away from the resort. Take a tour of St. Thomas, stopping off at Mountain Top for a famous banana daiquiri, or visit Charlotte Amalie, explore Blackbeard's Castle, and enjoy the town's world-class duty-free shopping.

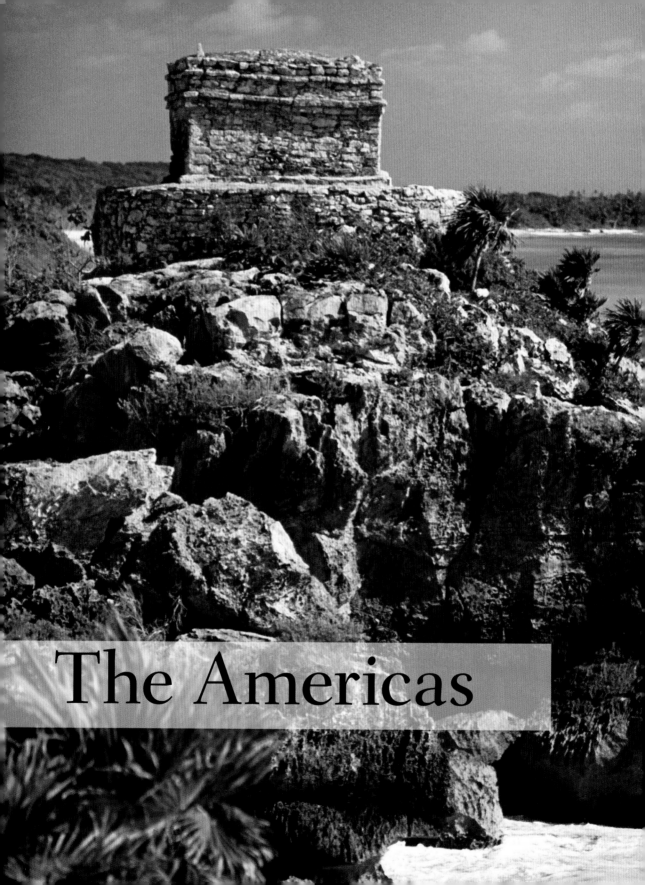

The Americas

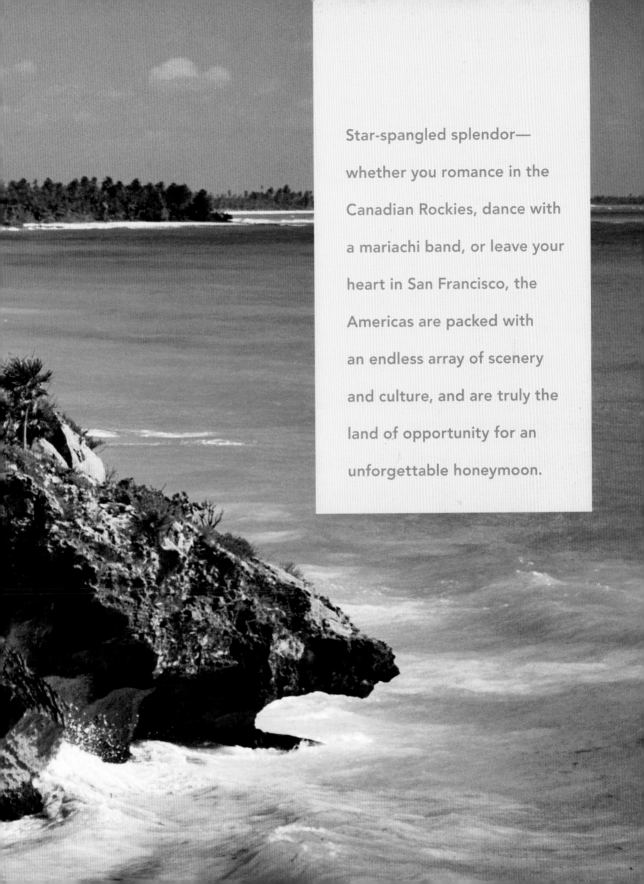

Star-spangled splendor—
whether you romance in the
Canadian Rockies, dance with
a mariachi band, or leave your
heart in San Francisco, the
Americas are packed with
an endless array of scenery
and culture, and are truly the
land of opportunity for an
unforgettable honeymoon.

the fairmont chateau lake louise

LAKE LOUISE

CANADIAN ROCKIES

"the romantic Rockies"

Mother Nature dealt a winning hand to the legendary Canadian Rockies. Imagine a backdrop of snow-topped towering mountains and turquoise lakes that changes its mantle with each season. From a winter wonderland scene of powder-soft snow, frozen lakes, snow-kissed peaks, and icicle-bedecked waterfalls, to a vista of green mountainsides and sunny meadows filled with wild flowers—the seasonal transformation of the Rockies is amazing. For couples seeking a majestic setting this is the place to say "I do."

If you're dreaming of an unusual wedding, or a honeymoon coupled with the ultimate in luxury and natural beauty, then Alberta's Rocky Mountains are the answer to your prayers.

The Rockies offer a magnificent natural environment, plus the promise of adventure, and they are graced with all the magical elements for the perfect romantic getaway or an action-packed vacation.

Alberta is home to endless idyllic locations and amenities to fulfill your every dream. For a winter wedding you'll be transported to a fairytale snowy land where you can snuggle up under soft blankets and embark on a horse-drawn sleigh ride, ice skate hand in hand on sparkling Lake Louise, experience the thrill of dog-sledding, or try out the runs at world-renowned ski resorts.

In the summer months you can walk through meadows studded with wildflowers on the shores of emerald glacier-fed lakes, ride on horseback through mountains or prairies, or even try whitewater rafting.

VITAL STATISTICS

rooms 550 rooms/suites

email chateaulakelouise@fairmont.com

website www.fairmont.com

legal requirements

- Prior to the wedding ceremony an Alberta marriage license must be obtained from a registry in the province of Alberta. For further details contact the Canadian Embassy or Consulate in your nearest city

documents required

- Passport
- Full name and birthplace of father; full name, birth name, and birthplace of mother
- Divorce decree if divorced
- Death certificate of former spouse if widowed

ABOVE

The roofed private balcony of a Belvedere Suite offers breathtaking views of Lake Louise.

—

LEFT

Horseback riding in the Rockies is available during the summer months.

—

FAR LEFT

Wedding receptions can be held in the Sun Room looking over the spectacular glacier.

BRIDAL FILE

- *Onsite wedding coordinator*
- *3 wedding packages*
- *Weddings take place in several function rooms, the Victoria Terrace, the Ice Castle (December to March only)*
- *Ceremony conducted by a celebrant or minister*
- *Transportation: horse-drawn carriage, horse-drawn sleigh, canoe, horseback*
- *Music: local musicians playing traditional native music, harpist, local choir, solo classical/modern singer, taped music, organ/piano, string trio/quartet, folk musicians*
- *Spa, gym, hair salon*
- *Hair stylist, beautician, masseur*
- *Photographer & videographer*
- *Individually designed cake*
- *Flowers & boutonnieres*
- *Floral table decorations*
- *Separate room for the bride and groom to prepare for the wedding*
- *Valet service*

The Fairmont Chateau Lake Louise is only a two-hour drive west from Calgary on the banks of a breathtaking lake and embraced by snow-frosted mountains. Tucked deep within Banff National Park, it provides a retreat for lovers where they can escape to an atmosphere of welcoming grandeur.

ABOVE

The majestic Rocky Mountains provide an astounding backdrop to the chateau and lake.

Built in 1890, this heritage property known as "The Diamond in the Wilderness," retains its feeling of old-world charm and elegance. It's easy to see why the chateau has played host to royalty and the famous over the years.

The 550 rooms and suites have views over Lake Louise. Nineteenth-century styling graces every furnishing, with king-size beds, cloud-soft comforters, and luxurious fabrics. Windows open to let in the crisp, fresh mountain air.

For total relaxation and pampering, the soothing surroundings of the Escape Spa & Salon are highly recommended after a day in the great outdoors.

Dining at the chateau provides a memorable experience with a choice of five restaurants offering both local and international cuisine. The Fairview Dining Room has views that outshine its refined china and elegant menus, while the Victoria Room restaurant, with its glowing chandeliers and stone fireplaces, is pure regal splendor.

Lake Louise is a matchless scene for any wedding. There's an onsite wedding coordinator and weddings are tailored to the individual couple.

Marriages can take place in several grandiose salons, or on the Victoria Terrace, a private area elevated from the hotel grounds with spectacular views of the lake and glacier. From December to March there's the choice of the Ice Castle, which stands on the frozen lake.

After the ceremony, what could be more idyllic than to take an old-fashioned horse-drawn sleigh ride along the shores of the lake before enjoying a romantic dinner in your suite or in one of the renowned restaurants?

Whatever the season, there are plenty of adventures to be had and a plethora of amazing sights to see in this heaven on earth known as "the romantic Rockies."

ABOVE
Intricate ice carvings decorate the chateau's grounds in winter.

———

BELOW
Plush Junior Suites invite you to lean back and drink in the view.

royal hideaway playacar
QUINTANA ROO
MEXICO

"a dream come true"

From the Caribbean Sea in the east to the Pacific Ocean in the west, Mexico is a land steeped in history and natural beauty. Azure ocean waters, mountainous terrain, and serene sandy beaches are juxtaposed with grand haciendas and awe-inspiring sites from the Mayan dynasty. Picturesque towns and beautiful colonial cities contrast sharply with mangrove swamps and forests. Explore deserts, party day and night, or whale-watch at some of the best sites in the Pacific Ocean. Whatever you decide, Mexico will amaze you.

RIGHT

Lanterns light the way to your beachside dinner for two.

———

FAR RIGHT

The Mexican colonial splendor of the Royal Hideaway Playacar.

———

BOTTOM RIGHT

The casual elegance of the Junior Suites.

Whether your idea of heaven is relaxing on a secluded stretch of sand, playing water sports from dawn to dusk, or taking time out for a romantic stroll amid some ancient ruins, you are sure to find it in Mexico.

Thousands of years ago, the Mayans and Aztecs were attracted to the Mexican coastline by its irresistible beaches, gemstone waters, and dry, sunny climate.

Today sun-lovers still head there for precisely the same reasons, only life on the beautiful sun-drenched and secluded beaches of the Mayan Riviera is more exciting and more luxurious than ever before.

Magnificent world-class hotels line the palm-fringed coast, parasailers and windsurfers jazz up the shore, and those ever-perfect days melt into steamy nights filled with dancing under the stars.

The Royal Hideaway Playacar is only one hour from Cancun in 13 acres of lush, tropical gardens on one of the most stunning beaches on the Yucatan Peninsula. This is the ultimate wedding and honeymoon destination.

Inspired by the beauty of the natural world, the Royal Hideaway Playacar will immerse you in a sophisticated tropical ambience with its perfect blend of Mexican and Spanish colonial architecture and casual, stylish design.

The 200 rooms and suites are filled with every comfort and luxury, from snug bathrobes and slippers, and pillows of your choice, to mouthwatering chocolates, freshly cut flowers, and candles.

The decor is a perfect combination of dramatic, dark wood furniture with bright, tropical touches that provide a soothing Zenlike mood that inspires romance and relaxation.

Each of the six exceptional restaurants offer samples of the world's finest delicacies in an atmosphere of refined elegance, while the romantic at heart will enjoy dining alfresco at the grill, or privately on the beach.

The hotel's first-class spa is the perfect place to unwind and offers the finest in spa, beauty, and body treatments, whereas the beachfront decks by the cascading infinity pool are just the spot to stretch out and enjoy the sun.

VITAL STATISTICS

rooms 200 rooms/suites

email weddings@mx.occidentalhotels.com

website www.royalhideaway.com

legal requirements

- To marry in Mexico, couples are required to have a blood test
- As ceremonies are conducted in Spanish, couples may need to arrange for an interpreter
- Religious marriages are not recognized under Mexican law
- Once the ceremony has been conducted, couples need to obtain a copy of the marriage certificate to have it apostilled (certified by a special letter and stamp) so the marriage is legally recognized on return to their own country
- For further details of legalities, contact the Mexican Embassy or Consulate in your nearest city

documents required

- Passport
- Birth certificate
- Divorce decree if divorced
- Death certificate of former spouse if widowed
- Legal proof if name has been changed

Royal Hideaway weddings are a dream come true. There are several different packages and an onsite wedding coordinator who will make sure that your wedding is exclusive and that no other marriages will take place on your special day.

Marriages are held on the beach, in the gardens, or in the garden gazebo. They are conducted by a Justice of the Peace, and a Mexican mariachi band gives your wedding a true local flavor. As ceremonies are conducted in Spanish, couples may need to arrange for an interpreter to be present.

ABOVE

The Relax pool with secluded terraces and shaded groves.

——

TOP RIGHT

Say "I do" under a flower-bedecked gazebo.

——

RIGHT

Enjoy Italian dishes and regional delicacies at the Palazzo restaurant, with its elegant and charming atmosphere.

After the ceremony you can celebrate by enjoying a romantic moonlight extravaganza beach dinner before returning to your suite to find it decorated with flowers, some chilled champagne and a hot tub filled with rose petals.

If you can bear to tear yourself away from the hotel, then there's plenty to see and do. Visit ancient Mayan ruins or Playa del Carmen, a quaint picturesque fishing village with all types of arts and crafts, and sidewalk cafés for people-watching.

BRIDAL FILE

- *Onsite wedding coordinator*
- *Wedding packages*
- *Weddings take place on beach, in garden, or in garden gazebo*
- *Ceremony conducted by Justice of the Peace*
- *Music: local musicians playing Mexican songs, mariachi band, violinist, guitarist, saxophonist, flutist, CD*
- *Spa, gym, hair salon, beauty salon*
- *Hair stylist, beauty therapist, masseur*
- *Photographer & videographer*
- *Individually designed cake*
- *Flowers*
- *Floral table decorations*
- *Separate room for the bride and groom to prepare for the wedding*
- *Valet service*

biltmore
MIAMI
FLORIDA

"a wedding at the Biltmore allows you to select the setting of your dreams"

A tropical paradise with sun-kissed days, white-sand beaches, world-class hotels, and a pulsating nightlife, Miami is the ideal place for a romantic getaway. Settle into a suite, sip a sunset drink with your feet in the sand, stroll under the stars along the boardwalk, or take a moonlight cruise through hidden waterways. Pack a picnic and while away the day eating chocolate-dipped strawberries under the shade of sweet-smelling ylang-ylang trees or sample gastronomic elegance under towering palms at a romantic restaurant.

For where else in the world do fabulous beaches lie right next to one of the most exciting urban centers on earth? Couple this with its weather, unbelievable scenery, beautiful people, and contagious vitality, and your love affair with Miami will begin.

Explore the historic and "happening" Art Deco District, spot alligators in the Everglades, enjoy ballet or opera, windsurf over the ocean, sip Cuban coffee, take a cigarette boat across the bay, dive to a coral reef, touch parrots and porpoises, dance and feast your way through a street festival, or just lose yourself on a serene sandbar—Miami can be exactly what you want it to be.

Miami is noted for its world-class hotels. The famous Biltmore hotel is set against a subtropical sky above the verdant Coral Gables landscape, where shady palm trees frame the curving boulevards.

ABOVE

All of the luxury rooms and suites feature European feather bedding and fine Egyptian cotton duvet covers.

From its earliest history Miami, with its rich subtropical landscape, sun, sand, and beautiful bays, has attracted a diverse group of seekers and dreamers.

Visit this vibrant cosmopolitan city and you will immediately understand why.

VITAL STATISTICS

rooms 280 rooms/47 suites

website www.biltmorehotel.com

legal requirements &
documents required

- Marriage regulations differ for Florida and non-Florida residents. For details, check with the Miami-Dade County Courthouse
- Birth certificate (if a minor)
- Passport, driver's license, or photo ID
- Social Security number
- Exact date of last divorce, death of spouse, or annulment if either applicant has been previously married

First opened in 1926, the Biltmore counted the Duke and Duchess of Windsor, Judy Garland, the Roosevelts, and the Vanderbilts among its guests, and the legendary gangster Al Capone took up residence in the Everglades Suite. Today it still plays host to presidents, movie stars, and a host of celebrities.

The hotel is set on 150 acres of gardens and its atmosphere reflects the grandeur of the Jazz Age. Its historic charm and Mediterranean architecture can be seen in the cathedral arches, hand-painted ceilings, intricate chandeliers, antique mirrors, and exclusively designed furnishings.

BELOW

Daytime or nighttime, Florida's landmark resort is always a spectacular sight.

211

The 280 rooms and 47 suites are luxurious, cozy, and welcoming. Bathed in natural light from oversize picture windows, they have comfortable sitting areas with custom-designed wood furnishings, and king-size beds.

The Biltmore provides a unique restaurant experience. Dine at the 1200 Courtyard Grill or head inside to Palme D'Or where gourmet dining is at its very best. The Cascade Poolside Bar & Grill is perfect for casual alfresco meals.

The famous Biltmore pool, the largest in a hotel in the U.S., was the scene of gala aquatic shows in the 1930s and is frequently used as a backdrop for movies and fashion shoots. Its lush landscaping, waterfall, and private cabanas make it the ideal place for relaxation.

A wedding at the Biltmore allows you to select the setting of your dreams. Choose from a ceremony by a sparkling fountain in the courtyard, on a terrace, or in the romantic garden or spectacular ballroom.

The hotel has an onsite wedding coordinator, and ceremonies are conducted by ordained clergy or those so authorized by the State of Florida.

Make a grand arrival in a horse-drawn carriage, or take an idyllic ride through the tree-lined streets of Coral Gables after the ceremony, before experiencing a romantic dinner for two in the restaurant of your choice, or in your suite.

BRIDAL FILE

- *Onsite wedding coordinator*
- *Ceremony conducted by ordained clergy or those so authorized by the State of Florida*
- *Weddings take place in ballrooms, terraces, courtyards, or poolside*
- *Transportation: horse-drawn carriage*
- *Music: to suit couple's choice*
- *Spa, gym, hair salon*
- *Hair stylist, beautician, masseur*
- *Photographer & videographer*
- *Individually designed cake*
- *Flowers*
- *Floral table decorations*
- *Separate room for the bride and groom to prepare for the wedding*

During your stay there's plenty to do in the area. Explore South Beach, the place to see and be seen in, visit Miami's Little Havana with its sidewalk cafés and aroma of hand-rolled cigars, explore the famous Coconut Grove, a haven for writers, artists, and the rich and famous, or just take a sunset cruise and enjoy champagne and canapés as the mystical Miami sun sets.

LEFT

The spa pampers the body, mind, and spirit.

———

OPPOSITE TOP LEFT

The Biltmore is the only luxury golf and spa resort in Miami, and has the largest outdoor pool in a hotel in the U.S.

———

OPPOSITE LEFT

Romantic dining by the fountain in the 1200 Courtyard Grill.

———

BELOW

Walk hand in hand through beautifully landscaped gardens.

pink shell beach resort & spa
FORT MYERS
FLORIDA

"an idyllic island location"

Powder-white sand, warm sunshine, exotic hideaways, and a chance to indulge yourself in fantasy—the Sunshine State is the perfect spot for your wedding. Experience some of the best sunsets in the world on moonlight beaches, cruise the tranquil warm ocean waters, meander through lush botanical gardens, or find a romantic escape on one of the secluded islands around the coast—the Sunshine State will fulfill every couple's dream.

From vibrant cities to sprawling national parks, nothing can compare with the diversity that Florida has to offer.

Journey through relaxing coastal towns, take in the spectacular Everglades, visit historic houses, or experience the magic, fun, and fantasy of Disneyworld. The choice is yours.

Along the Gulf of Mexico on Florida's southwest coast you'll find Fort Myers, a bustling town with a long and checkered history. For more than 200 years visitors have been coming to the town, including Thomas Edison, who loved it so much he bought a house there and later persuaded his friend Henry Ford to buy the house next door. The two houses are now local history museums and are well worth a visit.

Fort Myers is the gateway to a stretch of islands, some accessible only by boat and known for their natural beauty and pristine shell-strewn beaches.

ABOVE

Steal a kiss by the shore.

———

FAR LEFT

Relax in a beachfront suite.

———

LEFT

A signature Pink Shell
wedding cake.

———

BELOW

Fort Myers Beach—the
perfect place to chill out.

The most popular is Fort Myers
Beach, where you will find the Pink
Shell Beach Resort & Spa, an idyllic
island location.

Set in 12 acres of beautiful gardens
with a large expanse of powder-white
sand, lapped by the gentle waves of
the Gulf of Mexico, this luxurious resort
in a quiet location has everything you
could want for the perfect wedding and
honeymoon destination.

The 225 beachfront villas, with their
own open-air screened patios looking
out over the gulf, are furnished in
tropical elegance. There are separate
living and dining areas, with sofas to
relax on, king-size beds and every
amenity for your comfort, while some
villas have hot tubs and walk-in showers.

The hotel's leisure facilities include
three heated swimming pools and
water sports and boat rental facilities.
Cruises depart regularly from the hotel's
private dock.

VITAL STATISTICS

rooms 225 villas/suites

email weddings@Pinkshell.com

website www.pinkshell.com

**legal requirements &
documents required**

- Marriage regulations differ for Florida
  and non-Florida residents. For details,
  check with the Miami-Dade County
  Courthouse
- Birth certificate (if a minor)
- Passport, driver's license, or photo ID
- Social Security number
- Exact date of last divorce, death of
  spouse, or annulment if either applicant
  has been previously married

For pure pampering the world-class Aquagёne Spa has the latest treatments including a special couple's massage.

The two full-service restaurants provide the best in both local and international cuisine. Poolside Bongo's Bar and Grill is the perfect option for those sultry honeymoon nights.

At the Pink Shell Beach Resort & Spa weddings are a specialty with an onsite wedding coordinator and several packages.

Weddings are performed by a licensed officiant and can take place on the White Sands Beach. This offers the bride the chance of a grand entrance down a staircase onto the pool deck and out along the boardwalk.

For couples who prefer an indoor wedding the beautiful Captiva Ballroom

BELOW

Take in the view while relaxing on the terrace.

RIGHT

One of the swimming pools
at the Pink Shell.

—

BOTTOM RIGHT

Indulge yourself in the
tranquil Aquagëne Spa.

BRIDAL FILE

- *Onsite wedding coordinator*
- *Wedding packages*
- *Ceremonies are held on beach, or in ballroom*
- *Ceremony conducted by licensed officiant*
- *Transportation: horse-drawn carriage, vintage car, open-top car*
- *Music: to suit couple's choice*
- *Spa, gym*
- *Beauty therapist, manicurist, masseur, makeup artist*
- *Separate room for the bride and groom to prepare for the wedding*
- *Valet service*

External suppliers can be suggested for the following:

- *Hair stylist*
- *Photographer & videographer*
- *Individually designed cake*
- *Flowers*
- *Floral table decorations*

has big picture windows looking out onto the clear waters of the Gulf of Mexico. Its stylish veranda offers a wonderful view of the setting sun and the night sky filled with millions of stars.

After the wedding there are lots of adventures to be had. Take a shelling and nature boat trip, or a sunset cruise, visit some of the historical sites in the area, or just enjoy the amazing facilities that this resort has to offer.

the inn at perry cabin
ST. MICHAELS
MARYLAND

"the perfect wedding venue and honeymoon hideaway"

Snuggle up in front of a roaring fire in your mountain cabin, or wake up to the sound of seagulls after spending the night in a beach resort. Pack a picnic and experience the beautiful views of green pastures and cloud-topped mountains, or hop aboard a boat and enjoy a sunset cruise. Maryland is made for romantics and is the perfect place to exchange your vows.

Take a leisurely stroll, sun yourself on golden beaches, swim in the Atlantic Ocean, travel through the Allegheny Mountains, or sail across the great Chesapeake Bay—Maryland is a wonderful wedding and honeymoon destination waiting to be discovered.

You'll find lively ports, gracious towns, and exciting cities, including the storybook colonial capital, Annapolis. There's "a step back in time" atmosphere here, and to get the most out of the place, let a costumed guide take you around the cobbled streets and brick sidewalks where many of the buildings are more than 200 years old.

Annapolis is home to the United States Naval Academy and much of the movie *An Officer and a Gentleman* was shot here.

Maryland's historic past is reflected in Chesapeake Bay towns such as St. Michaels. Take a horse-drawn

carriage tour to experience the relaxed pace of this quaint resort on the Eastern Shore dating back to the mid-1600s, with its boutiques, antiques shops, restaurants, and museums, amid restored homes with Victorian exteriors.

ABOVE AND BOTTOM RIGHT

Intimate and exclusive, the Inn at Perry Cabin has been designed as a contemporary take on a Maryland seaside inn.

Enjoy the beauty and romance of the mansion waterfront—the perfect setting for your wedding.

Set in a 25-acre estate on the waterfront is the The Inn at Perry Cabin. This 19th-century colonial mansion, steeped in history, is the perfect wedding venue and honeymoon hideaway.

The 78 elegant rooms and suites of The Inn at Perry Cabin are just as you would imagine them to be. Most rooms have French doors that lead onto a deck, patio, or veranda. Furnishings are a mix of modern and period furniture. Upholstered sleigh or traditional wooden bedsteads are piled high with pillows and tastefully dressed with soft eiderdowns.

The restaurant, Sherwood's Landing, has been awarded accolades for its food and service. Sample the local dishes, including Chesapeake crab, Hayman sweet potato, and the inimitable Maryland Cookie at afternoon tea-time.

Swim in the heated outdoor pool, work out in the gym, or take a bicycle made for one or two and set off on your own adventure. Alternatively, enjoy a spot of pampering at the Linden Spa or just stretch out on the lawn with a glass of chilled wine and watch the world go by.

the waldorf-astoria
NEW YORK CITY
NEW YORK

"the quintessential luxury hotel experience"

In "the city that never sleeps" diversity, culture, and style are intensified. Experience those sublime New York moments by wandering down Fifth Avenue, soaking up the avant-garde atmosphere of Greenwich Village, strolling around Central Park, or walking through Times Square. The energy and fast pace of life in this city is perfect for couples seeking an exciting destination for their special day.

Immortalized in fiction and on film, New York with its fast-paced energy and myriad attractions has become one of the world's most famous wedding hot spots.

The Big Apple entices couples with its legendary wedding locations and incredible landmarks, the very names of which stir excitement.

BRIDAL FILE

- *Onsite wedding coordinator*
- *Weddings take place in 38 different venues, including Empire and Hilton Rooms, Grand Ballroom, Starlight Roof, Louis XVI and Conrad Suites*
- *Ceremony conducted by wedding officiant*
- *Transportation: horse-drawn carriage, vintage or open-top car*
- *Music: to suit couple's choice*
- *Spa, gym, hair salon*
- *Hair stylist, beauty therapist, manicurist*
- *Photographer & videographer*
- *Invidually designed cake*
- *Flowers & boutonnieres*
- *Floral table decorations*
- *Separate room for the bride and groom to prepare for the wedding*

It's impossible to experience all that this city has to offer, but no visit to New York would be complete without seeing the iconic Statue of Liberty and Empire State Building. Go to the top in the late afternoon to see the city by day and then catch it all lighted up for evening. Or linger after dinner on the observation deck, open until midnight.

Leave some time for shopping in the world-famous department stores or walk up Madison Avenue from 59th to 72nd Streets, where you can explore the exclusive stores. Remember to take an extra bag for all your purchases.

Downtown, there's SoHo, with its stylish art galleries, boutiques, and bistros housed in historic cast-iron buildings along cobblestone streets. In Midtown on the East Side enjoy the grandeur of the art deco Chrysler Building and the restored Grand Central Terminal, the perfect place for a bite of lunch.

ABOVE

Unashamed luxury in the Presidential Suite.

—

LEFT

The grandeur of the Park Avenue lobby.

—

BELOW

The majestic art deco exterior.

On Park Avenue you'll find one of the first "grand hotels"—the famous Waldorf–Astoria. World-renowned for over three-quarters of a century, the art deco landmark is the epitome of grandeur, style, and opulence. With its luxurious elegance and air of nostalgia, this is the ultimate place to tie the knot.

The hotel has a fascinating history and has played host to royalty and the rich and famous since its grand opening. Princess Grace and Prince Rainier of Monaco had their engagement party in the celebrated Conrad Suite. The Royal Suite was the private residence of the Duke and Duchess of Windsor for more than ten years, and the Presidential Suite has been the New York home to every U.S. president since Hoover.

VITAL STATISTICS

rooms 1,416 rooms/suites

website www.waldorf.com

legal requirements

- A New York State marriage license, available from the Office of the City Clerk in New York City. Couples will be asked for identification and evidence they are free to marry, if either has been married before

documents required

- Driver's license or passport
- If divorced, divorce decree may be needed

Frequently the scene of glittering social events, the hotel has also been the backdrop for numerous classic movies and TV productions.

The Waldorf-Astoria's 1,416 rooms and suites epitomize the quintessential luxury hotel experience. Each spacious, individually decorated room and suite is furnished with timeless elegance and classic sophistication.

Innovation and tradition meet at the hotel's celebrated restaurants, bars, and lounges. From a classic steakhouse and American brasserie to an acclaimed Japanese restaurant, the Waldorf-Astoria entices diners with its creativity and culinary distinction.

LEFT

A traditional, formal wedding.

—

BELOW

Have your first dance together as husband and wife in the dazzling Grand Ballroom.

—

RIGHT

The Silver Corridor is crowned with elegant chandeliers.

—

BELOW RIGHT

Relax in one of the Waldorf-Astoria's lobbies.

A dedicated team of wedding coordinators at the hotel will help craft your fairytale wedding. Venues include the elegant splendor of the Empire and Hilton Rooms, the intimacy of the Conrad Suite, the dazzling opulence of the Grand Ballroom, and the Starlight Roof, with its gilded ceiling, crystal chandeliers, and magnificent views of Manhattan.

After the ceremony you can savor a sumptuous dinner in the private dining area of the Peacock Alley restaurant, or you can enjoy the 24-hour room service and have dinner served in your suite.

the fairmont
SAN FRANCISCO
CALIFORNIA

"a tribute to time, elegance, and grace"

San Francisco is full of iconic images—those little cable cars climbing halfway to the stars, the scarlet slash of the Golden Gate Bridge, and the dragon-adorned gateway to Chinatown. Affectionately known as the "City by the Bay," it's a place of amazing contrasts and cultural diversity. From exclusive hilltop neighborhoods and beatnik haunts dating back to the 50s, to marinas, parkland, and waterfronts lined with seafood stalls—San Francisco is the destination with a difference.

BELOW

The Fairmont Suite on the 23rd floor accommodates functions for up to 75 people and has its own spacious bedroom.

San Francisco has been immortalized in songs, on the silver screen, and in countless best-selling novels as an exciting and romantic destination.

The city is built on a hilly peninsula between the Pacific Ocean and San Francisco Bay, which gives it its legendary foggy weather.

At the northern point is the city's most famous landmark, the Golden Gate Bridge, linking San Francisco to the Napa Valley wine country.

Sight-seeing the city by tram is a great way to navigate the steep hills and enjoy the spectacular views. There are also some good beaches, and some great restaurants and shops on Fisherman's Wharf.

As a fun-loving city, San Francisco enjoys an amazing nightlife with many bars, clubs, and theaters, plus colorful festivals and parades.

Set on the top of Nob Hill is the crown jewel of San Francisco, The Fairmont. As much a part of the city as the famous bridge, this legendary hotel is a tribute to time, elegance, and grace.

Built in 1907, the hotel has been host to the most remarkable events in San Francisco history. In the famed Venetian Room, Tony Bennett first sang "I Left My Heart in San Francisco."

In 1945, delegates from 40 countries met in the Garden Room to draft the charter of the United Nations.

The grandeur of The Fairmont is reflected in the 591 elegant, luxuriously furnished and individually decorated rooms and suites with their impressive views of the city and the bay.

The Fairmont has two fabulous restaurants, one of which, The Tonga Room & Hurricane Bar, offers its diners an unusual dining experience.

Here Pacific Rim Asian cuisine is served in a tropical setting that includes thunder and rainstorms.

The warmth and charm of The Fairmont provide the ideal backdrop for weddings. The hotel has an onsite wedding coordinator and couples can choose their own wedding officiant.

There's a dazzling choice of locations, including the Gold Room with its ornate gold-leaf decoration, crystal chandeliers, indoor balconies, and hand-painted murals.

BELOW

Admire the view from the private rooftop terrace of the Penthouse Suite.

The Penthouse Suite has sweeping city and bay views from its terrace, and on the top floor of the hotel's Tower is the magnificent Crown Room. Especially designed for weddings, its wraparound windows give a 270-degree panorama of the Golden Gate and Bay Bridges, Coit Tower, Alcatraz, Downtown, and the Twin Peaks.

After your ceremony you can indulge in fine dining in the Laurel Court Restaurant & Bar, take advantage of

VITAL STATISTICS

rooms 591 rooms/suites

email sfreservations@fairmont.com

website www.fairmont.com

legal requirements

- A California State marriage license available from the Office of the County Clerk. Couples will be asked for information if either has been married before. You need at least one witness

documents required

- A legal picture I.D. card or passport
- If divorced, divorce decree may be needed
- If widowed, death certificate of former spouse may be needed

ABOVE

The magnificent setting of the Gold Room.

———

BELOW

Relax and take in the view of the landscaped roof garden.

BRIDAL FILE

- *Onsite wedding coordinator*
- *Weddings take place in a number of venues, including Venetian Room, Crown Room, Gold Room and Penthouse Suite*
- *Ceremony conducted by officiant of couple's choice*
- *Transportation: horse-drawn carriage, vintage or open-top car*
- *Music: to suit couple's choice*
- *Spa, gym, hair salon*
- *Hair stylist, beautician, masseur*
- *Photographer & videographer*
- *Individually designed cake*
- *Flowers & boutonnieres*
- *Floral table decorations*
- *Separate room for the bride and groom to prepare for the wedding*
- *Valet service*

an in-room candlelight dinner for two, or take a romantic cruise on the calm waters of San Francisco Bay.

During your honeymoon there are plenty of things to do.

Take a trip to the Napa Valley wine country, board a ferry and visit Alcatraz, or get tickets for a vintage movie, the ballet, or opera at one of the many arts venues in the city.

LEFT
The Penthouse Suite has its own library.

litchfield plantation
PAWLEYS ISLAND
SOUTH CAROLINA

"gracious living in a secluded setting"

Sunny beaches, crystal lakes, historic towns, and scenic mountains—South Carolina is not just a place, it's an adventure. Ride in a horse-drawn carriage down tree-lined streets, passing quaint houses that date back to the 1700s. Stroll hand in hand along pristine beaches, explore fascinating barrier islands, or enjoy the tasteful seclusion of staying in a whitewashed colonial-style plantation house. Graced with every ingredient for the perfect wedding and honeymoon, South Carolina possesses a romantic Old South charm.

One of the original colonies with a rich history and culture shaped by European, African, and Caribbean influences, South Carolina offers a charming setting for a wedding.

The broad beaches of the Grand Strand stretch for some 60 miles along the northern coast and are edged with sand dunes and sea oats. Historic Charleston is a fascinating city full of old-world charm and picturesque pastel-colored buildings with decorative iron gates and manicured lawns.

A short drive away you'll find Pawleys, a 3.5-mile-long island with a laid-back atmosphere and an unspoiled beach. The earliest known inhabitants of the area were the Waccamaw and Winyah Indians. They called the area "Chicora," meaning "the land," and the term is frequently used by locals even today.

ABOVE

The private marina.

—

LEFT

Drinks for two in the guest house bar.

VITAL STATISTICS

rooms 32 rooms/retreat cottages

email vacation@litchfieldplantation.com

website www.litchfieldplantation.com

legal requirements

- A South Carolina State marriage license.
  Wedding packages include license
  and transportation to and from the
  license bureau. Couples will be asked
  for identification and evidence they are
  free to marry, if either has been married
  before

documents required

- A legal picture I.D. card or passport
- Divorce decree if divorced
- Death certificate of former spouse
  if widowed

Litchfield Plantation is on Pawleys
Island, nestled between ancient rice
fields and pristine beaches. Set on
600 acres, it's an 18th-century sanctuary
surrounded by majestic moss-draped
oaks and flowering dogwoods and
azaleas.

During the 1700s and 1800s
Litchfield was a working rice plantation
with land extending from the Waccamaw
River to the Atlantic Ocean. In the 1970s
it was converted to a secluded resort.

ABOVE

Relax by the fire in the
Carriage House Library.

BRIDAL FILE

- *Onsite wedding coordinator*
- *3 wedding packages*
- *Weddings take place on beach or in a shady oak grove*
- *Ceremony conducted by member of the clergy or officer authorized to administer oaths in South Carolina*
- *Transportation: horse-drawn carriage, vintage or open-top car*
- *Music: local musicians playing traditional music, local choir, solo classical/modern singer, taped music, organ/piano, string trio/quartet, folk musicians/singer*
- *Spa, gym, hair salon*
- *Hair stylist, beauty therapist, manicurist, masseur, makeup artist*
- *Photographer & videographer*
- *Individually designed cake*
- *Flowers*
- *Floral table decorations*
- *Separate room for the bride and groom to prepare for the wedding*

The white plantation house stands at the end of an avenue of oak trees and could almost have come from the pages of a romantic novel. The last remaining plantation house in coastal Georgetown County, this property is made for romantics.

There are just 32 rooms and retreat cottages on the site. Rooms and suites abound with Southern charm and offer an escape that many only dream of. The Ballroom Suite is perfect for honeymooners with its large living area, four-poster king-size bed, fireplace, and bathroom with an oversize whirlpool tub for two. It has a wonderful view over the plantation grounds.

BELOW

The Avenue of Oaks is a perfect place to enjoy a romantic stroll.

RIGHT

Four-poster luxury, Southern style, in the Gun Room Suite.

FAR RIGHT

Breakfast with a view in the Summer Drawing Room.

BOTTOM RIGHT

Couples can wed in a shady oak grove.

Renowned for its fine food, the hotel's Carriage House Club restaurant is a fabulous dining experience, with magnificent views, antique furnishings, and paintings. From hearty plantation breakfasts with eggs Benedict and Low Country dishes and traditional afternoon tea to romantic dinners, the restaurant offers a high standard of mouthwatering specialties.

The property has a large free-form heated pool with views of the rice fields, two tennis courts, and a private marina.

Weddings at Litchfield Plantation are expecially romantic. There is an onsite wedding coordinator and you have a choice of three wedding packages.

Ceremonies, on the beach or in a shady oak grove, are conducted by a religious or civil official. And to give your special day a touch of the splendor of the Old South, weddings can include a horse-drawn carriage ride and a candlelight dinner at the Carriage House Club.

After the wedding there's plenty to do and see around the area. Take a jeep safari to Myrtle Beach, tour Charleston, take a waterways boat tour, watch a theater performance, or just enjoy the Southern legacy of gracious living at the Litchfield Plantation.

Index

A

activities *see under* individual destinations
Arajilla Retreat, Australia **70**
  activities 73
  bridal file 73
  ceremonies 72
  documents required 72
  island setting 70
  legal requirements 72
  retreat facilities 71–3
Ardanaiseig Hotel, Scotland **110**
  activities 113
  bridal file 112
  ceremonies 113
  documents required 110
  hotel facilities 112–13
  legal requirements 110
  West Highland setting 110–11
Ashford Castle, Ireland **100**
  activities 102–3
  blessing ceremonies 102–3
  bridal file 102
  County Mayo area 100–101
  documents required 100
  hotel facilities 101–2
  legal requirements 100

B

beauty, bridal
  exercise 26
  hair and beauty services 12
  hands 26
  relaxation techniques 26
  skin care 26, 27, 28, 29
  therapists 55
best man 45
Biltmore, United States **210**
  activities 213
  bridal file 213
  ceremonies 212–13
  documents required 211
  hotel facilities 211–13
  legal requirements 211
  Miami area 210
blessing ceremonies 102–3, 106–7
  see also ceremonies
bouquets, bridal 30–1
bridal files 54–55
  see also under individual destinations
bride *see* beauty, bridal; bouquets, bridal
bungalow accommodation 125, 151

C

cakes, wedding 33, 55
Carrington Resort, New Zealand **178**
  activities 181
  bridal file 181
  ceremonies 180
  documents required 180
  legal requirements 180
  North Island area 178–9
  resort facilities 179–80
catering 33

ceremonies
  conducted by 54
  legalities 38
  planning 38–9
  the special day 39
  see also under individual destinations
Château de la Chèvre d'Or, France **96**
  activities 98
  bridal file 98
  ceremonies 98
  documents required 99
  French Riviera setting 96–7
  hotel facilities 98–9
  legal requirements 99
city atmospheres 64, 67, 76, 92, 104–5, 147, 225–7
climate
  hair care 28
  heat, ways to beat 29
  underwear 22–3
  wedding ceremony 39
  see also weather
clothing 16
contraception 14
cottage accommodation 234
Crown Beach Resort, Cook Islands **132**
  bridal file 133
  ceremonies 134
  documents required 134
  tropical island setting 132–3
  legal requirements 134
  resort facilities 133–4

D

deep vein thrombosis 14
destinations
  checklist 49
  choosing 8–9, 45
  bridal files 54–5
  gifts 36–7
  weather in 56–7
  see also under individual destinations
diet 28
divorced couples 12
documents required
  see under individual destinations
dresses, wedding 19, 20–2

E

exercise 26

F

facials 27
Fairmont, United States **228**
  activities 231
  bridal file 231
  ceremonies 229
  documents required 230
  hotel facilities 229–31

C (Couran)

Couran Cove Island Resort, Australia **80**
  activities 81–3
  bridal file 81
  ceremonies 82
  documents required 83
  island setting 81
  legal requirements 83
  resort facilities 81–2

legal requirements 230
San Francisco area
228–31
Fairmont Chateau Lake
Louise, Canada 200
activities 201, 203
bridal file 202
ceremonies 203
chateau facilities 203
chateau setting 202–3
documents required
201
legal requirements 201
Rocky Mountain setting
201
figure, bridal
swimwear 24
wedding dresses 22
flowers 12, 30–1, 55
food 33
food hygiene 14
French Riviera 56, 96–7
friends, presence of
10–12, 45, 48

G

gifts 36–7
grooms 25
gym 55

H

hair care
climate 28
services 12
hairstyle 28
hairstylists 46, 55
hats, packing 19
health precautions
food hygiene 14
immunization/
vaccination 14

insect repellent sprays
15
long-haul flights 14
sun awareness 15
Hemingways Resort, Kenya
60
bridal file 63
ceremonies 62
documents required 62
legal requirements 62
resort facilities 61, 62
tropical coast setting 60
wildlife and safaris
60, 63
Hotel Cipriani, Italy 104
blessing ceremonies
106–7
bridal file 107
city setting 104–5
documents required
105
hotel facilities 106
legal requirements 105
Hotel Kämp, Finland 92
activities 95
bridal file 94
ceremonies 94
city setting 92
documents required 95
hotel facilities 93–4
legal requirements 95
Hotel Katikies, Santorini,
Cyclades Islands,
Greece 138
activities 141
bridal file 140
ceremonies 141
documents required
141
hotel facilities 139–40
island setting 138–9
legal requirements 141

I

Icehotel, Sweden 114
activities 117
bridal file 116
ceremonies 114
documents required 117
hotel facilities 116–17
legal requirements 117
magical setting 114–15
immunization 14
Inn at Perry Cabin,
United States 220
activities 221, 223
bridal file 223
ceremonies 222
documents required
222
hotel facilities 221
legal requirements 222
Maryland area 220
insect repellent sprays 15
InterContinental
Aphrodite Hills Resort
Hotel, Cyprus 142
activities 145
bridal file 145
ceremonies 145
documents required
143
hotel facilities 144–5
legal requirements 143
romantic setting 143–4

L

Labriz Silhouette,
Seychelles 182
activities 185
bridal file 185
ceremonies 185
documents required
184

legal requirements 184
resort facilities 183–4
tropical island setting
182–3
language obstacles 12
Le Manoir aux Quat'
Saisons, England 86
activities 89
bridal file 86
ceremonies 88–9
Cotswold setting 86
hotel facilities 88–9
legal requirements 9, 38,
39, 45, 46
see also under individual
destinations
LeSport, St. Lucia 186
activities 189
bridal file 189
ceremonies 189
documents required
187
legal requirements 187
resort facilities 187, 189
treatments 186
tropical island setting
186
licenses 9
lingerie 22–3
Litchfield Plantation,
United States 232
activities 235
bridal file 234
ceremonies 235
documents required
233
hotel facilities 234–5
legal requirements 233
Pawleys Island area
232–3
long-haul flights 14, 29

Longueville Manor, Jersey,
Channel Islands **128**
   activities 131
   bridal file 130
   ceremonies 131
   documents required
     131
   hotel facilities 129–31
   island setting 128–9
   legal requirements 131

M

makeup 17, 29, 46
makeup artists 55
malaria 14, 15
manicurists 55
marriage announcements
  42
marriage certificates 38
masseurs 55
moisturizers 27
Montpelier Plantation Inn,
Nevis **174**
   activities 177
   bridal file 176
   ceremonies 177
   tropical island setting
     174–5
   inn facilities 176–7
Mount Nelson Hotel, South
Africa **64**
   bridal file 66
   ceremonies 67
   city setting 64, 67
   documents required 65
   hotel facilities 65, 67
   legal requirements 65
music, choice of 32, 46, 54

O

Observatory Hotel,
Australia **76**
   activities 79
   bridal file 78
   ceremonies 79
   city setting 76
   documents required 77
   hotel facilities 78–9
   legal requirements 77
One&Only Le Saint Géran,
Mauritius **164**
   activities 167
   bridal file 167
   ceremonies 167
   documents required
     166
   tropical island setting
     164–5
   legal requirements 166
   resort facilities 165–6
One&Only Ocean Club,
Bahamas **120**
   activities 123
   bridal file 122
   ceremonies 122
   documents required
     122
   hotel facilities 122–3
   tropical island setting
     120–1
   legal requirements 122
Outrigger on the Lagoon,
Fiji **150**
   bridal file 153
   ceremonies 152
   documents required 151
   tropical island setting
     150, 151
   legal requirements 151
   resort facilities 151–2

P

packing
   cosmetic products 17
   hats 19
   organization of 18
   shoes and clothes
     16–17, 18
   wedding wardrobe 17,
     47
parents 45, 48
passports 45
pavilion accommodation
  183
perfumes 29
photographers 12, 34–5,
  39
photographs 25, 34–5, 43
Pink Shell Beach Resort &
Spa, United States **214**
   activities 217
   bridal file 217
   ceremonies 216, 217
   documents required
     215
   Florida area 214–15
   legal requirements 215
   resort facilities 215–6
post-nuptial celebrations
  42–3
pre-nuptial dinner 48
preparations countdown
  44–8
Princeville Resort, Hawaii
154
   activities 157
   bridal file 157
   ceremonies 157
   documents required
     156
   tropical island setting
     154–5

   legal requirements 156
   resort facilities 147–8
purses 16–17

R

relatives, presence of
  10–11, 45, 48
relaxation techniques 26
Round Hill Hotel, Jamaica
160
   activities 162–3
   bridal file 163
   ceremonies 162
   documents required
     162
   tropical island setting
     160
   legal requirements 162
   resort facilities 161–2
Royal Hideaway Playcar,
Mexico **206**
   activities 209
   bridal file 209
   ceremonies 208
   documents required
     208
   hotel facilities 207
   legal requirements 208
   tropical coast setting
     206–7

S

second marriages 12
Sheraton Grande Laguna,
Phuket, Thailand **190**
   activities 193
   bridal file 192
   ceremonies 193
   documents required
     191

tropical island setting 190

legal requirements 191

resort facilities 190, 192–3

shoes 16, 25

skin care 26, 27, 29

Southern Cross Club, Cayman Islands 124

activities 127

bridal file 127

ceremonies 127

club facilities 125–6

documents required 125

tropical island setting 124

legal requirements 125

spas 54

speeches 43

sun awareness 15, 26

swimwear 24

T

Taj Exotica Resort & Spa, Mauritius 168

activities 171

bridal file 171

ceremonies 171

documents required 169

tropical island setting 168

legal requirements 169

resort facilities 168, 170, 171

toiletries 17

transportation 32, 47, 54

U

underwear 22–3

V

vaccination 14

valet service 55

videography 35, 43, 55

villa accommodation 133, 148, 161, 165, 170, 179, 184, 190, 192, 215

visas 45

Viva Wyndham Samaná, Dominican Republic 146

activities 149

bridal file 147

ceremonies 148

documents required 149

tropical island setting 146, 147

legal requirements 149

resort facilities 148

W

Waldorf-Astoria, United States 224

bridal file 225

ceremonies 227

documents required 226

hotel facilities 226

legal requirements 226

New York City area 225–7

wardrobe see wedding wardrobe

weather

Bahamas 56

British Isles 56

Canadian Rockies 56

Cape Town 56

Cayman Islands 56

Channel Islands 56

Cook Islands 56

Cyclades Islands, Greece 56

Cyprus 56

Dominican Republic 56

Fiji 56

Finland 56

Florida 56

French Riviera 56

Hawaii 56

Jamaica 57

Jersey see Channel Islands

Kenya 57

Lord Howe Island 57

Maryland 57

Mauritius 57

Mexico 57

Nevis 57

New York 57

New Zealand 57

Phuket, Thailand 57

St. Lucia 57

San Francisco 57

Santorini see Cyclades Islands

Seychelles 57

South Carolina 57

South Stradbroke Island 57

Sweden 57

Sydney 57

U.S. Virgin Islands 57

Venice 57

wedding cakes 33, 55

wedding coordinators 9, 38, 39, 45, 47, 54

wedding dresses 19, 30, 31

wedding gifts 36–7

wedding packages 9, 38, 54

wedding wardrobe

choosing 20–5, 45, 46

grooms 25

packing 19

post-nuptial party 43

swimwear 24

underwear 22–3

wedding dresses 20–2

widowed couples 12

witnesses 39

Wyndham Sugar Bay Resort and Spa, U.S. Virgin Islands 194

activities 197

bridal file 195

ceremonies 197

documents required 196

tropical island setting 194–5

legal requirements 196

resort facilities 195–6

Acknowledgments

The Automobile Association wishes to thank the following photographers and companies for their assistance in the preparation of this book.

Abbreviations for the picture credits are as follows – (t) top; (b) bottom; (l) left; (r) right; (c) centre; (AA) AA World Travel Library

3 Stockbyte; 4 Ingram; 4–5 Tina Baumgartner/FOTOLIA; 6–7 Stockbyte; 8 (t) AA/Peter Baker, (b) AA/Steve Watkins; 9 (t) AA/Clive Sawyer, (bl) AA/Jim Carnie, (br) AA/Steve Day; 10 Courtesy of Pink Shell Beach Resort & Spa; 11 Brand X Pictures; 12–13 Stockbyte; 14 Digital Vision; 15 Courtesy of The Observatory Hotel; 17 & 18 (t) Photodisc; 18 (b)–19 Stockbyte; 20 Brand X Pictures; 21 (c) & (t) Brand X Pictures, 21 (b) Stockbyte; 22–23 Stockbyte; 24 Triumph Swimwear; 25 Stockbyte; 26 Courtesy of The Taj Exotica Resort & Spa, Mauritius www.tajhotels.com; 27 (l) Bananastock, (r) Brand X Pictures; 28 (t) Stockbyte, (b) Brand X Pictures; 30 Brand X Pictures; 31 (t) Ingram, (b) Stockbyte, (r) Kyle Rothenborg/Courtesy of Princeville Resort; 32 Courtesy of Pink Shell Beach Resort & Spa, 32 (b) Brand X Pictures; 33 (l) Photodisc, 33 (c) & (r) Ingram; 34 Stockbyte; 35 (t) Ingram, (b) Brand X Pictures; 36 Ingram; 38 (t) Brand X Pictures, (b) Stockbyte; 39 Brand X Pictures; 40–41 Stockbyte; 42 Ingram; 43 Photodisc; 44 Brand X Pictures; 46 Ingram; 47 Brand X Pictures; 48 Ingram; 50–51 AA/Clive Sawyer; 57 Alexey Kotelnikov/Fotolia.com; 58–59 AA/Paul Kenward; 60–63 Courtesy of www.slh.com Hemingways Resort in Kenya is part of Small Luxury Hotels of the World except 60 (tl) & 61 (t) Kenya Tourist Board www.magicalkenya.com; 64–67 Courtesy of Mount Nelson Hotel, Cape Town, South Africa & Orient-Express Hotels, Trains & Cruises; 68–69 AA/Paul Kenward; 70–73 Courtesy of Arajilla.com.au except 70 (t) Jack Shick; 74–75 AA/Paul Kenward; 76–79 Courtesy of The Observatory Hotel & Orient-Express Hotels, Trains and Cruises; 80–83 Courtesy of Couran Cove Island Resort; 84–85 AA/Anna Mockford & Nick Bonetti; 86–89 Courtesy of Le Manoir aux Quat' Saisons except 89 (b) Stockbyte; 90–91 AA/Hugh Palmer; 92 (t) Superclic/Pictures Colour Library; 92(b)–94 Palace Kämp Group & Orient-Express Hotels, Trains & Cruises; 95 Finnish Tourist Board; 96–98 Courtesy of Le Château de la Chèvre d'Or; 100–103 Courtesy of Ashford Castle; 104–107 Orient-Express Hotels, Trains & Cruises; 108–109 AA/Jonathan Smith; 110–113 (t) Courtesy of Ardanaiseig Hotel, 113 (b) Brand X Pictures; 114 (t) Bengt Jaegtnes, (b) Big Ben/Artist: Daniel Rosenbaum; 115 (l) Big Ben 2007/Artist: Jorgen Westin, (r) Big Ben 2007/Artists: Rashid Sagadeev & Leonid Kopeykin; 116 Haken Hjort; 117 Big Ben/Artists: Mikael Nille Nilsson, Mark Armstrong & Ake Larsson – all courtesy of The ICEHOTEL; 118–119 Southern Cross Club, Marc Montocchio www.hydraulicphoto.com; 120 (t) John Henebry, (b) Bruce Wolf; 121 (t) Bruce Wolf, (b) Maura McEvoy; 122 MacDuff Everton; 123 Bruce Wolf – all courtesy of www.oneandonlyresorts.com; 124–127 Southern Cross Club, Marc Montocchio www.hydraulicphoto.com; 129 (b) Damon Eastwood www.visualeyedesign.com; 130 (b) Stockbyte; 132 (t), 133 (t), 134 (t), 135 (t) – all courtesy of Cook Islands Tourism Corporation www.cook-islands.com; 132 (c) & (b), 133 (b), 134 (b), 135 (b) – all courtesy of www.crownbeach.com; 136–137 AA/Terry Harris; 138–141 Courtesy of www.katikies.com; 142–145 Courtesy of www.aphroditehills.com Aphrodite Hills Resort and InterContinental Aphrodite Hills Resort Hotel, Cyprus; 146–147 (t) & 148 (t) Courtesy of Viva Wyndham Samaná, 147 (b) Photodisc; 148 (b) AA/Clive Sawyer; 149 (t) Lee Karen Sawyer, (b) Stockbyte; 150–153 Courtesy of Outrigger on the Lagoon, Fiji; 154 (t) Warren Jagger, (b) Kyle Rothenborg courtesy of Princeville Resort; 155 (t) & (b) Warren Jagger courtesy of Princeville Resort; 155 (c) Hawaii Tourism Europe www.hawaii-tourism.co.uk; 156–157 Warren Jagger – all courtesy of Princeville Resort; 158–159 Courtesy of Princeville Resort; 160 & 161 (t) Courtesy of Round Hill Hotel/David Massey, 161 (b) Round Hill Hotel/Tim Larsen-Collinge; 162 Round Hill Hotel/Tim Larsen-Collinge; 163 (t) Round Hill Hotel/David Massey, (b) Round Hill Hotel/Alan Smith; 164 (t) & 167 (b) Barbara Kraft, 164 (t), 165 & 166 Dan Ham, 167 (t) Anthony Osmond-Evans; 168–173 Courtesy of The Taj Exotica Resort & Spa, Mauritius www.tajhotels.com; 178–181 Courtesy of Carrington Resort/Gareth Eyres except 179 (t) Jody Ranby; 182–185 Courtesy of www.slh.com Labriz Silhouette in the Seychelles is part of Small Luxury Hotels of the World; 190–193 Courtesy of Kylie Brajak, Director of Sales and Marketing, Sheraton Grande Laguna; 194–197 Courtesy of Wyndham Sugar Bay Resort & Spa; 198–199 AA/Peter Wilson; 200–205 Courtesy of Fairmont Hotels and Resorts; 210–213 Courtesy of the Biltmore; 214–217 Courtesy of Pink Shell Beach Resort & Spa; 218–219 AA/Jon Davison; 220–223 Josh Gibson, Orient-Express Hotels, Trains and Cruises except 220 (t) Frank Edwards, Orient-Express Hotels, Trains & Cruises; 224–227 Courtesy of The Waldorf-Astoria except 224 (t) Courtesy of NYC & Company; 228–231 Courtesy of The Fairmont, San Francisco except 228 (t) AA/Ken Paterson; 232–235 Courtesy of www.litchfieldplantation.com.

Every effort has been made to trace the copyright holders, and we apologise in advance for any unintentional errors. We would be pleased to apply any corrections in any future edition of this publication.

The author and publisher are grateful to the following for permission to reproduce copyright material:

Hemingways Resort, Kenya www.hemingways.co.ke
Mount Nelson Hotel, Cape Town, South Africa www.mountnelson.co.za
Arajilla Retreat, Lord Howe Island www.arajilla.com.au
Couran Cove Island Resort, South Stradbroke Island www.couran.com
The Observatory Hotel, Sydney www.orient-express.com
The InterContinental Aphrodite Hills Resort Hotel, Cyprus www.aphroditehills.com, www.intercontinental.com/aphrodite
Le Manoir aux Quat' Saisons, England www.manoir.com
Hotel Kämp, Finland www.hotelkamp.fi
Château de la Chèvre d'Or, French Riviera www.chevredor.com
Ashford Castle, Ireland www.ashford.ie
Hotel Cipriani, Venice www.hotelcipriani.com
Ardanaiseig Hotel, Scotland www.ardanaiseig.com
Icehotel, Sweden www.icehotel.com
One&Only Ocean Club, Bahamas www.oneandonlyresorts.com
Southern Cross Club, Cayman Islands www.southerncrossclub.com
Longueville Manor, Jersey, Channel Islands www.longuevillemanor.com
Crown Beach Resort, Cook Islands www.crownbeach.com
Hotel Katikies, Santorini, Cyclades Islands, Greece www.katikies.com
Viva Wyndham Samaná, Dominican Republic www.vivawyndhamresorts.com
Outrigger on the Lagoon, Fiji www.outrigger.com
Princeville Resort, Hawaii www.princevillehotelhawaii.com
Round Hill Resort, Jamaica www.roundhilljamaica.com
One&Only Le Saint Géran, Mauritius www.oneandonlyresorts.com
Taj Exotica Resort & Spa, Mauritius www.tajhotels.com
Montpelier Plantation Inn, Nevis www.montpeliernevis.com
Carrington Resort, North Island, New Zealand www.carrington.co.nz
Labriz Silhouette, Seychelles www.slh.com/labrizsilhouette
LeSport, St. Lucia www.thebodyholiday.com
Sheraton Grande Laguna, Phuket, Thailand www.luxurycollection.com/phuket
Wyndham Sugar Bay Resort & Spa, U.S. Virgin Islands www.wyndham.com
The Fairmont Chateau Lake Louise, Canadian Rockies www.fairmont.com
Royal Hideaway Playacar, Mexico www.royalhideaway.com
Biltmore, Florida www.biltmorehotel.com
Pink Shell Beach Resort & Spa, Florida www.pinkshell.com
The Inn at Perry Cabin, Maryland www.perrycabin.com
The Waldorf-Astoria, New York www.waldorf.com
The Fairmont, San Francisco www.fairmont.com
Litchfield Plantation, South Carolina www.litchfieldplantation.com

With special thanks to:
Ruth Atkinson - editorial
Diane Winkleby - americanisation/editorial
Also Mel Watson - picture research